WINNING THE DRUG WAR

A Twentieth Century Fund Paper

Winning the Drug War

A National Strategy

by Mathea Falco

PP Priority Press Publications/New York/1989

HV 5825 .F34 1989
Falco, Mathea.
Winning the drug war

Library of Congress Cataloging-in-Publication Data
Falco, Mathea.
  Winning the drug war.

  "A Twentieth Century Fund paper."
  Bibliography: p.
  Includes index.
  1. Narcotics, Control of—United States.
I. Title.
HV5825.F34   1989   363.4'5'0973   89-14603
ISBN 0-87078-263-0
ISBN 0-87078-262-2 (pbk.)

Foreword

The United States is in the midst of a drug epidemic. The manifestations are myriad—babies born addicted to drugs overfill our cities' public hospitals, drug wars ravage parts of the nation's capital, and the criminal justice system flounders under an unprecedented number of drug-related cases. Policy recommendations also are myriad. Calls for legalization follow closely on appeals for tougher sentencing. Those advocating greater funding for education—the "just say no" campaign, for example—are countered by those arguing that the money would be better spent on interdiction.

The failure to devise a coherent drug-fighting strategy is in part the result of the complexity of the issues involved. It is also a function of the political process—politicians respond to public outrage and demands for immediate action with short-term solutions. Nevertheless, Mathea Falco, former assistant secretary of state for international narcotics matters, argues that Congress now has two opportunities to engage in a serious review of the nation's drug policies: The first is offered by the Gramm-Rudman-Hollings Budget Deficit Act, which should force critical examination of current drug programs—and provide the impetus to jettison those that have not proven effective. The second is the presentation of William Bennett's national drug control strategy this September.

In reformulating the nation's war on drugs, Falco argues, Congress must acknowledge the need for multiple efforts in research, prevention, enforcement, and treatment programs. Further, there must be acceptance of the fact that certain programs may take a long time to accomplish their goals; failure to demonstrate immediate success should not result in their abandonment. For example, it may take years before prevention and education programs produce demonstrable results; this potentially useful weapon in the war against drugs should be protected during the interim from the vagaries of the political system.

We believe that Falco has made an important contribution to the national debate over drug policy. We are grateful to her for it.

Marcia Bystryn, ACTING DIRECTOR
The Twentieth Century Fund
June 1989

Contents

For Bethuel M. Webster (1900-1989)

Chapter 1

Introduction

National polls now indicate that Americans rate drug abuse as the nation's most important domestic and foreign policy problem, more serious even than the budget deficit and arms control. The polls also show that an overwhelming majority disapproves of the job the federal government has been doing to combat illegal drugs. Public concern has reached new levels of intensity, sustained by daily, highly visible media coverage of the drug problem. As a result, drug abuse has become a key issue in recent elections; candidates of both parties warn that the war on drugs has not been won and that greater efforts are needed.

There are a number of reasons for this current national preoccupation. The rapid spread of the potent cocaine derivative "crack" since its emergence in 1985 has had a dramatic impact both on patterns of drug abuse and on drug trafficking. Unprecedented increases in violent crime by users as well as traffickers have stretched an already overburdened criminal justice system and left many citizens fearful for their own safety. Recent evidence that the AIDS virus is spreading most rapidly among intravenous drug users has further intensified public fear.

Concern with drug use in the workplace has also increased, particularly in relation to jobs that directly affect public safety such as train conductors and airline pilots. In addition, drug-related absenteeism affects productivity, and, at a time when many Americans feel increasing vulnerability to foreign economic competitiveness, the far-reaching effects of drug abuse seem to corrode our capacity to respond to the challenges of the future. The failure of President Ronald Reagan's eight-year "national crusade" against drugs has deepened public pessimism; there is a widespread sense that effective governmental action against drug abuse may not be possible.

There has been surprisingly little public debate on what the goals of a national drug policy should be or how they might be implemented. This may be due in part to the complexity of the issue and the lack of easy answers. Public outrage has increased the pressure for immediate action, reducing the likelihood of longer-range conceptual planning. Moreover, the problems of drug abuse and trafficking are closely tied to the deeper structural problems of poverty, race, education, and employment opportunity in our society. As a result, no drug policy, however effective, can by itself eliminate drug abuse, but thoughtful measures may be able to reduce the damage substantially.

Congress adopted two major anti-drug abuse acts prior to the 1986 and 1988 elections, which together authorized funding of $6.5 billion. However, neither piece of legislation was preceded by comprehensive congressional hearings; instead, the bills reflected a series of last-minute political compromises. In 1989, Congress has two unusual opportunities to review national drug policy and seriously discuss priorities.

The first opportunity will arise in connection with appropriations for the 1988 Anti-Drug Abuse Act. When the act was adopted in October 1988, only $500 million of the authorized $2.7 billion in new funding could be made available for expenditure in 1989 because of budgetary constraints imposed by the Gramm-Rudman-Hollings Budget

Deficit Act. If the act is to be fully funded, Congress will have to take funds from other nondrug programs or increase taxes. These tough choices among competing priorities should force Congress—and the country—to examine the goals and effectiveness of present drug control strategies.

A second opportunity for review of national drug policy has arisen in connection with President Bush's newly appointed "drug czar," William Bennett, who was President Reagan's outspoken secretary of education. He directs the new Office of National Drug Policy Control created by Congress in the 1988 Anti-Drug Abuse Act (after years of opposition by the Reagan administration). The office has broad programmatic and budgetary review authority over the many federal agencies currently involved in the anti-drug effort. For the first time there is a single, cabinet-level official responsible for drug policy. The director is required to submit to Congress a national drug control strategy, including recommended budget levels, by September 1989. If Congress actively engages Bennett over the formulation of this strategy, which will be revised annually, it could become a major vehicle for public debate over national drug policy.

Can the United States devise a realistic framework for a national policy that addresses the reduction of both the demand for and supply of illicit drugs? An important first step is to describe present trends in drug use and abuse and place them in the perspective of the past twenty-five years, including the historical context in which the nation's drug laws developed. It is also instructive to contrast the U.S. approach with the experience of European countries in dealing with drug abuse.

A review of U.S. drug control strategy for the past two decades, and particularly the past eight years, reveals patterns that explain the present sense of crisis. By now we have learned quite a lot about what works—and what does not—in reducing demand through education, prevention, and treatment, as well as about reducing illicit drug supplies through law enforcement. Against this background, it is possible to formulate an effective national strategy to combat drug abuse and drug trafficking.

Chapter 2

Defining the Drug Problem

When most Americans express concern about the drug problem they think primarily of illicit drugs—marijuana, heroin, and cocaine. These drugs have traditionally been the major targets of federal drug control policy and will be the focus of this paper. However, it is important to remember that misuse of legal drugs—alcohol, tobacco, and psychoactive prescription drugs—causes many more deaths each year and costs the nation far more in lost productivity, health problems, and property loss than do illegal substances. Yet, for historical reasons (discussed later), American attitudes toward these legal drugs have differed sharply from their views on heroin, cocaine, and marijuana. These differences have had a powerful impact in shaping policy.

The fact is that there is no single drug problem; rather, there is a nationwide problem with drugs. The vast majority of those who abuse illicit drugs are also heavy consumers of legal substances, including alcohol and tobacco. And while heroin, cocaine, and marijuana are the most widely used illegal drugs, different cities and different populations also experience severe problems from other substances. In Washington, D.C., and Los Angeles, for example, PCP (phencyclidine) abuse is widespread and is the cause of recent increases in hospital emergency room admissions and overdose deaths.

Extent of Illicit Drug Use in America

Illicit drug use is pervasive. Nearly 60 percent of all teenagers try an illicit drug before they finish high school, and use is occurring at increasingly early ages.[1] More than 23 million Americans use drugs regularly; of these, 10 to 20 percent are believed to use them daily.[2] Although use has declined slightly during the past decade, the United States still has the highest rate of illegal drug use and abuse of any industrialized country in the world.

Not surprisingly, illegal drugs present an increasing problem in the workplace. The number of employers who identified drugs and alcohol as significant problems in their organizations increased by 20 percent from five years ago.[3] These employers estimate that absenteeism, medical expenses, and lost productivity cost an average of 3 percent of their total payroll. General Motors, for example, reported that substance abuse among its 472,000 workers and dependents cost the company $600 million in 1987. The National Institute of Drug Abuse (NIDA) estimates that lost productivity from illicit drug use costs the nation more than $33 billion a year.

Our knowledge about the extent of national illicit drug use is limited.[4] Information comes entirely from voluntary interviews, which probably means underreporting actual use, and reports only on seniors in high school or people living in households. Many at high risk for drug abuse (school dropouts—who are disproportionately male, black or Hispanic, and from the inner city—truants, and individuals not living at a fixed address or in jails and other institutions) are not reached. Drug use among this population is hard to measure, but estimates from arrest and hospital emergency room data show they are much more likely to use crack and heroin than those interviewed in national surveys. Because of the limitations on both the type of reporting and the samples interviewed, the actual extent of illicit drug use—especially among adolescents—is probably significantly higher than the surveys indicate.

Despite these limitations, however, certain broad trends in illicit drug use and abuse over the past twenty-five years are clear:

- Adolescents are trying alcohol, tobacco, and drugs at ever younger ages, even as drug use (especially daily use of marijuana) has generally declined since 1980. Cocaine use by high school seniors began to decline in 1987.
- Adult drug use has also decreased, except for cocaine. Heroin use is most difficult to measure—estimates are that the number of addicts has remained constant in the past decade at about half a million.
- Most of the marijuana and cocaine consumed in the United States is used by a relatively small percentage of the population.

The trend, then, is encouraging. Illicit drug use among both adolescents and adults nationwide has been declining gradually since the beginning of the decade. Cocaine has been the exception, although the most recent data on high school seniors indicate that cocaine has lost considerable popularity among this group.

Reduced drug availability has apparently not been a factor in the overall decline.[5] Rather, concerns about health and increased awareness of the dangers posed by drugs seem to be the major deterrents, along with economic factors and future aspirations. Teenagers whose parents have some graduate education report a greater decline in illicit drug use than those whose parents have not finished high school; teenagers who plan on going to college report substantially less drug use than those who do not. (See appendix to this chapter for further discussion of trends in illicit drug use.)

The picture that emerges from the national surveys on drugs suggests an increasingly divided America. Illicit drug use remains a problem for all social, economic, and ethnic groups in our society, but less so among the affluent. The encouraging downward trend of the past decade has been most pronounced among middle-class, educated Americans. Heroin addiction continues to be concentrated among poor minorities; crack has become epidemic in the nation's inner cities. Calls to the national Cocaine Help Line reflect this trend. In 1983, more than half the calls for help came from university-educated people earning at least $25,000 a year. By 1987, more than half the calls came from people who were unemployed; only 15 percent were university educated.

The poor and disadvantaged suffer the multiple consequences of drug abuse and trafficking more grievously than the general population. They are at much greater risk for unemployment, AIDS, homelessness, and crime (either as victim or perpetrator). Their children are more likely to drop out of school or be placed in foster care. Treatment for drug abuse is less available to them than to those who are insured or can afford private programs. In particular, crack has increased the vulnerability of the poor not only to the devastating effects of drug addiction but also to the violence of the traffickers.

Crack

Crack, a far more concentrated form of cocaine, has become a national concern since 1985. More than any other drug in the past two decades, crack (named for the cracking sound it makes when smoked) has created a sense of crisis over the failure of drug policy. Medical and treatment experts agree that crack is particularly dangerous because of its pharmacology and its low cost. Its widespread use has given rise to unprecedented levels of violence; it has surpassed heroin as the drug of choice in the inner city, causing dramatic increases in homicides and other crimes. New York City police reported that, in 1986, homicides in northern Manhattan, where crack trafficking has been heavy, rose 22 percent, compared with a

9 percent drop in 1985. Drug-related killings in Washington, D.C., jumped from 50 in 1985 to 220 in 1988. In Los Angeles, where homicides had generally been declining, drug-related killings increased from 320 in 1985 to 450 in 1988.

Crack is easy to make and relatively inexpensive compared to cocaine. Cocaine sells for $80 to $100 a gram on the street while crack is sold in vials costing $3 to $15. Before crack, the only way to produce smokable cocaine ("freebasing") involved using highly flammable solvents and often resulted in explosions, like the one in which comedian Richard Pryor was severely burned. Crack smoking is a much safer process.

Crack, generally smoked in a water pipe or sprinkled on tobacco or marijuana, reaches the brain within seconds and immediately creates an extraordinarily intense euphoria that lasts ten to fifteen minutes. The sharp letdown that follows leaves users feeling depressed and anxious. Driven by a craving to recapture the "high," users become entrapped in a cycle of compulsive use and increasing need.

Cocaine, which is usually inhaled or "snorted," produces a less intense euphoria than crack. Its effects take longer to be felt and the letdown is more gradual; an addiction takes longer to develop. Treatment experts report that, while cocaine users often use the drug for four or five years before seeking help, crack users experience physical and psychological difficulties quickly, sometimes within weeks of first use.[6]

Crack users frequently experience cocaine psychosis, first described by Sigmund Freud in 1884 but never experienced by most cocaine users. Scientists believe that the psychotic symptoms are caused by the effect of cocaine on dopamine production, which rises suddenly when the drug enters the bloodstream and drops again when the drug wears off. When dopamine levels rise repeatedly, particularly in day-long binges of crack use, psychotic symptoms often develop.

Unlike heroin, which has a sedative effect, crack makes

users highly agitated, violent, and paranoid. The results are often unpredictable and tragic. For example, in January 1989, a 16-year-old New York City schoolchild without any previous criminal activity killed his mother because she would not give him $200 to buy crack. In 1988, another teenager killed five people and seriously wounded six others in a series of robberies while on a crack binge.

Crack has become particularly popular among women,[7] destroying many inner-city families in which women are the only parent. Reports of child abuse and neglect in New York City more than tripled—to 8,521 from 2,627—from 1985 to 1987 in cases where either mothers or both parents were drug users. During the same period, the number of babies born in New York City with illegal drugs in their urine jumped from 1,325 to 5,088. Over 80 percent of the women and 90 percent of the children with AIDS became infected as the result of direct or indirect contact with intravenous drug use. One in seventy-seven babies born in New York City in 1987 tested positive for HIV; most of those infected also tested positive for cocaine, and most were born to women who were drug users or partners of drug users.

New research on babies exposed to cocaine before birth has found that they can be severely damaged even with very little cocaine use by the mother. These babies show a wide range of ill effects, including retarded growth, neurological abnormalities, and even strokes. They tend to be smaller and have smaller heads and brains than normal babies; they are also at much greater risk of unexplained crib death.[8]

Drug Use and AIDS

Public concern about the damaging effects of drug abuse has been greatly compounded by recent evidence that the AIDS virus is spreading most rapidly among intravenous drug users. NIDA estimates that there are 1.1 to 1.3 million people in the United States who use needles to inject heroin, cocaine, and amphetamines. In New York City, which has more than 200,000 intravenous users, half the AIDS deaths between 1981 and 1986 were drug related. City officials estimate that 60 to 70 percent of the intravenous drug users are HIV-positive, which means that most of them will contract AIDS within the next ten years.

The so-called crack houses, where crack is used and sold and where sex is often exchanged for drugs, have recently emerged as major sources for AIDS infection because many users turn to heroin and other intravenous sedative drugs to bring them down slowly from the accelerated highs of crack. They use needles that are shared by dozens of other crack-house visitors.

The widespread risk from sharing needles poses dangers also for those who use drugs casually. Young people in particular, for whom drug experimentation is often a rite of passage, are placed in extreme danger from sharing needles even once. Although a single encounter may not result in drug dependence, it can infect the user with the fatal AIDS virus.

Drug Use and Crime

For many Americans, concern about drug abuse has become synonymous with fear of the unprecedented violence generated by drug traffic. Recent research confirms this perception that criminal activity and drug abuse are closely related.[9]

The term "drug-related crime" is used generally to mean either crimes arising from illicit drug sales and traffic; crimes intended to obtain money to buy drugs; crimes involving violent, erratic behavior provoked or exacerbated by drug abuse; or crimes of purposeful violence related to drug trafficking, like the gang murders in Los Angeles. All of these have increased substantially in recent years.

The total population in federal and state prisons currently exceeds 600,000, more than three times as large as it was in 1970. Convictions for violation of the drug laws are now the single largest and fastest-growing category in the federal prison population, comprising 35 percent of the total. (Robbery is second, at 15 percent.)[10]

Unlike the earlier traffic in heroin, marijuana, and other drugs, crack traffic has become a major employer of children. In many inner-city neighborhoods, teenagers process, package, and distribute the drugs while younger children serve as lookouts and messengers. The youngsters can earn several hundred to several thousand dollars a day, money usually spent on highly visible consumer goods (or, sometimes, shared with their often-impoverished families). Because the law treats these traffickers as juvenile delinquents rather than criminals, they are rarely detained for long.

The increases in drug-related juvenile arrests parallel those of the adult population. In New York City, juvenile arrests tripled from 1983 to 1987; in Washington, D.C., they almost quadrupled. Drug-related arrests for children under the age of 12 also increased significantly. The Los Angeles County juvenile justice system, originally designed for 1,300 children, now houses more than 2,000.[11]

It is clear that drugs, either directly or indirectly, affect an enormous range of the population. From babies to teenagers to adults, the consequences of this "scourge," to use President Bush's word, are evident in all sectors of society. Any definition of the population suffering from the drug problem would have to include us all.

APPENDIX

Illicit Drug Use among Young People

The first national survey on marijuana use was conducted by the National Commission on Marijuana and Drug

Abuse in September 1971. Using a limited national probability sample, the researchers found that 15 percent of the adults and 14 percent of the young people (ages 12–17) had used marijuana at some time. Five percent of the young people reported daily marijuana use, compared to 3 percent of the adults.

The National Commission conducted a more comprehensive survey in the fall of 1972. The survey found that, while almost half the young adults (ages 18–25) had used marijuana, experimentation by teenagers remained at 14 percent. In addition to marijuana, teenagers also reported trying LSD (4.8 percent), cocaine (1.5 percent), and heroin (0.6 percent).

The first national High School Senior Survey, conducted in 1975, reported that almost half the class had used marijuana. Over a fifth of the class had used stimulants; 9 percent had tried cocaine. By 1979, drug use in this group reached all-time highs: 60 percent had tried marijuana; 15 percent had used cocaine; and 24 percent had used stimulants. These trends among young people are also reflected in the National Household Surveys conducted in 1977 and 1979.

Since 1980, adolescent drug use has generally declined. This decrease has been most dramatic for daily drug use. By 1986, this figure had dropped to one in twenty-five. During the same time period, amphetamine use among seniors dropped to 5.5 percent from its peak of 13 percent in 1981. PCP, LSD, and heroin use among this group have remained quite low.

Among seniors, cocaine is now the second most widely used illicit drug after marijuana. However, for the first time this decade, the 1987 Senior High School Survey found that reported cocaine use dropped from 12.7 percent to 10.3 percent of the seniors. In 1988, use continued to drop—to 7.9 percent. Daily cocaine use declined from 0.4 percent in 1986 to 0.2 percent in 1988.

The use of the highly addictive cocaine derivative crack has also declined among high school seniors. The 1986 survey contained specific questions on crack for the first time. Of the one in six seniors who had ever used cocaine, 4.1 percent reported having tried crack. This percentage remained level in the 1987 survey, but dropped significantly—to 3.1 percent—in 1988.

Despite the encouraging evidence of a gradual decline in overall drug use among adolescents, studies show that children are trying alcohol, tobacco, and drugs at younger ages. The National Adolescent School Health Survey, conducted by the U.S. Public Health Service in 1987, found that use of alcohol begins as early as fifth grade, and by eighth grade, more than three-quarters of the students have tried it. One-quarter of them report having had five or more drinks at least once during the past two weeks. Tobacco use is almost as widespread: more than half the eighth-grade students and two-thirds of the tenth-grade students have smoked. The vast majority of them first tried cigarettes by the sixth grade.

In addition to the serious health consequences of tobacco and alcohol use among children, there is also evidence that their use becomes part of a pattern of progression in involvement with drugs, particularly marijuana. The 1987 National Adolescent Survey found that 15 percent of the eighth-grade students had tried marijuana, compared to 35 percent of the tenth-grade students. However, almost half the eighth-grade students who used marijuana reported their first use by sixth grade, while the older students reported first use by eighth grade.

This trend toward earlier experimentation with drugs is even more apparent with cocaine. Two-thirds of the eighth-grade students who had used cocaine (5 percent) first tried it by seventh grade. Three-quarters of the tenth-grade students who had used cocaine (9 percent) first tried it by ninth grade.

Illicit Drug Use among Adults

The gradual decline of illicit drug use among adolescents during the past decade is also reflected in the adult population. From 1979, the peak year for marijuana use among 18–25-year-olds, the percentage of those who tried marijuana decreased from 68 percent to 60 percent in 1985. Cocaine, the second most widely used illicit drug after marijuana, is an exception to this pattern. Population estimates based on the most recent (1985) National Household Survey show that the number of people who used cocaine in the month prior to the survey increased from 4.2 million in 1982 to 5.8 million. Most of this increase occurred among people aged 26 years or older.

Many Americans believe that illicit drug use is more prevalent among minority groups than among the general population. However, surveys report somewhat contradictory results on this point. The standard survey techniques used by the National Household Survey, which rely entirely on interviews with members of households, may not adequately reflect drug use by minorities in the inner cities.

The 1985 National Household Survey found significantly lower marijuana and cocaine use among blacks and Hispanics than among whites under the age of 35; blacks over the age of 35 reported higher rates. Information on heroin use showed that blacks reported a slightly higher rate than whites and substantially higher than Hispanics.

A much more limited survey conducted in 1988 by the Partnership for a Drug-Free America found that blacks are more likely to use illicit drugs than whites.[1] The survey was based on interviews with college students and people at malls and central-city locations across the country. Among blacks interviewed, 23 percent of the adolescents had tried marijuana by age 13, and 12 percent had tried cocaine, compared with 16 percent and 5 percent of whites, respectively. Black adults and children also reported much greater accessibility to marijuana, cocaine, and crack than whites: 16 percent of the black children (ages 9–12) and 34 percent of the adults, compared to 6 percent of the white children and 17 percent of the white adults, said cocaine is easy to obtain. Fuller demographic information will emerge from the 1988 National Household Survey; however, the greater exposure of urban black children to drugs, particularly cocaine and crack, is already clear.

Most of the marijuana and cocaine consumed in the United States is used by a small proportion of the population. The 1985 National Household Survey found that approximately half of all persons who ever used marijuana and two-thirds of those who ever used cocaine did so ten times or less. Among those who used marijuana in the month prior to the survey, nearly half did so on four days or less; 30 percent used marijuana on 5–19 days; and 22 percent used marijuana on 20–30 days.

Heroin use is much harder to measure than marijuana and cocaine, both because it is less prevalent and because the groups who are more likely to use it are generally not reached by the surveys. The National Narcotics Intelligence Consumers Committee (NNICC) estimated in 1981 that there were about half a million heroin addicts in the United States. This figure is believed to have remained relatively stable during the decade.[2]

Although heroin use is too rare statistically to measure reliably in general surveys, it has consistently been a major factor in overdose deaths and medical emergencies. From 1976 through 1985, heroin ranked second or third among the drugs most frequently mentioned in hospital emergency room visits reported in the Drug Abuse Warning Network (DAWN).[3] The DAWN data show that the average age of these heroin users increased from 27 years in 1976 to 32 years in 1985. Treatment data obtained from Client Oriented Data Acquisition Process (CODAP) and other sources indicate that the average age of heroin addicts has continued to increase by about six months a year, indicat-

Figure 2.A1

Trends In Cocaine-Related Hospital Emergencies Reported Through DAWN, 1983-1986

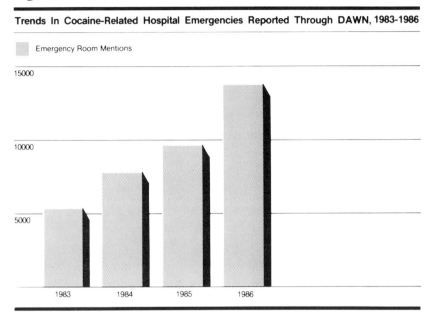

Note: The figure for 1986 was projected based on data for the first six months of that year.

Source: *The NNICC Report 1985-1986.*

ing that few new heroin addicts have been recruited since the mid-1970s.

Medical emergencies arising from cocaine use have increased dramatically in recent years. In 1981, cocaine was the sixth most frequently mentioned drug in hospital emergency room visits; by 1986, it was first, surpassing alcohol in combination with other drugs, which has traditionally been top ranked. During the same period, the number of cocaine-related hospital emergencies jumped from 3,095 in 1981 to 14,000 in 1986. (See Figure 2A.1.) Treatment data confirm the rapid increase in the harmful consequences of cocaine use. Between 1979 and 1984, the proportion of clients admitted for treatment of a primary cocaine problem increased from 3.9 percent to 14.7 percent.[4]

Chapter 3

The Historical Context:
The Origin of the Federal Drug Laws

Before the passage of the Harrison Narcotic Act in 1914 there were no legal restrictions on the sale of heroin, marijuana, or cocaine in the United States. In the late nineteenth and early twentieth centuries, these drugs were readily available over the counter in drugstores and grocery stores, as well as from doctors. Opium and cocaine were used in cough syrups, health tonics, patent medicines, and Coca-Cola. At the turn of the century there were an estimated 250,000 opiate addicts in the United States. Apart from Civil War veterans who had become addicted to morphine administered for pain, most of the addicts were women dependent on patent medicines. Despite their addiction, they were generally viewed as respectable if somewhat pitiable members of the community.

By the early 1900s there was public pressure to regulate these drugs. The first step was the passage of the Pure Food and Drug Act in 1906. Adopted in response to exposés of the patent medicine industry, the act required that manufacturers list ingredients on their labels. Public concern about opium smoking grew, particularly in California, with its large population of Chinese workers who had originally come to build the railroads. The United States took a leading role in developing the Hague Opium Convention of 1912, which pledged nations for the first time to control production and distribution of opium. (The Hague Convention was the foundation for a number of subsequent international narcotics-control agreements, leading to the Single Convention on Narcotic Drugs of 1961, the major international treaty governing their control.)

Partly in response to these international commitments, Congress in 1914 adopted the Harrison Narcotic Act, which imposed registration and record-keeping requirements on the production and sale of opiates and cocaine. By 1924, successive laws and legal interpretations of the act resulted in the prohibition of heroin production and importation into the United States. In 1937, marijuana was effectively prohibited under the Marijuana Tax Act.

Historians have noted that at the time of the passage of the drug laws, addiction was not widespread among the general population. The prohibited drugs were specifically associated with racial minority groups who were feared as potential sources of political and social unrest. Opium and heroin use were identified primarily with the Chinese; cocaine with blacks, particularly in the South; and marijuana with Mexican immigrants in the Southwest. Whatever humanitarian motives may have produced these laws, they also were an attempt to control the alleged lawlessness of the minorities who used them.[1]

Consequences for Drug Policy

The prohibitions on heroin, cocaine, and marijuana have been the cornerstone of U.S. drug policy since their adoption. It is important to note that they defined drug abuse primarily as a law enforcement problem rather than a health or social problem. Consequently, addicts have generally been seen as outlaws rather than as victims requiring help; the criminal justice system rather than the health-care system has been the dominant social framework for dealing with addicts.

The operative policy assumption ever since the passage of the Harrison Narcotic Act has been that effective enforcement of the drug laws will help reduce or eliminate drug abuse. This view has resulted in a primary role for enforcement in U.S. drug policy.[2]

By prohibiting drugs that were produced in other countries rather than manufactured domestically, the early U.S. laws in effect traced the origins of the drug problem to sources outside our borders, specifically to countries that failed to eliminate illicit drug production and traffic. As a result, international control efforts have been a critically important part of U.S. drug policy.

Historically, drug abuse has not been integrated into broader U.S. policy planning to combat developmental, social, and health problems. Until very recently, even the closely intertwined problems of drug and alcohol abuse were studied separately, reflecting profound differences in law and attitude toward the two groups of abusers (the United States being much more tolerant of alcoholics). Only since 1986, when Congress created the Office of Substance Abuse Prevention (OSAP), which addresses both drugs and alcohol, has there been bureaucratic recognition at the federal level of the commonality of many drug and alcohol problems. Congress gave OSAP responsibility for developing innovative approaches for the prevention of substance abuse. Separate from both the National Institute of Drug Abuse (NIDA) and the National Institute of Alcoholism and Alcohol Abuse (NIAAA), OSAP reports directly to the administrator of the Alcohol, Drug Abuse, and Mental Health Administration. It received an appropriation of $70 million in 1989.

The Changing Social Consensus in the United States

Even though the laws prohibiting heroin, cocaine, and marijuana have remained virtually unchanged for the past sixty years, social attitudes about these drugs have shifted considerably. Until the mid-1960s illegal drug use was not widespread, and most people generally accepted the prohibitionist approach. However, as marijuana use increased rapidly among young people in the late 1960s, the social consensus of earlier decades that deemed marijuana dangerous and undesirable began to change.

By the mid-1970s, efforts to decriminalize marijuana possession had taken hold. Ten states adopted decriminalization, and Alaska made marijuana possession legal. These changes reflected the view that marijuana users were not like other illegal drug users and did not belong in the criminal justice system. The changes also signaled increased social tolerance for marijuana as it came to be regarded as less dangerous than previously believed.

Cocaine use also increased in the mid-1960s but not as rapidly as marijuana. Relatively expensive at $100 a gram, cocaine became the status drug of choice among affluent professionals, sports stars, and entertainers. Extensive media coverage of cocaine use among the upper classes enhanced its glamorous image, its illegality notwithstanding.

The consensus that had reinforced drug prohibition since the 1920s held firm only with regard to heroin. The number of heroin addicts remained relatively constant during this period despite rapid increases in the number of other drug users.

Since 1980, accelerated by a resurgence of political conservatism, the consensus against marijuana and cocaine has strengthened. There has also been mounting medical and scientific evidence confirming the dangers of chronic marijuana use, particularly among adolescents. And cocaine, which had been considered by many in the medical community relatively benign compared to heroin, proved to be far more addictive and lethal than previously believed, particularly in its smokable form, crack. The cocaine-related deaths of sports stars Len Bias and Don Rogers in 1986 also hardened the attitudes of many Americans toward the drug.

In the 1970s most public debate focused on whether or not the prohibited drugs were dangerous; today, most Americans assume they are and focus instead on the appropriate policy response to a situation that is clearly out of control. The debate ranges from "zero tolerance" for any illicit drugs to legalization of all drugs.

Former First Lady Nancy Reagan, through her nationwide "Just Say No" campaign, has been a leading proponent of zero tolerance—the belief that any illicit drug use is criminal, regardless of circumstances or consequences. Mrs. Reagan's position is that casual drug users should be considered accomplices to murder because they keep drug traffickers in business. Users, like traffickers, should be subjected to severe criminal sanctions.

A diametrically opposite view proposes legalization in response to the failure of present drug policies. Proponents call for an end to the war on drugs, arguing that lifting the prohibition would greatly reduce crime related to sales and traffic, just as did the repeal of alcohol prohibition. They recognize that legalization might result in millions of Americans becoming drug-dependent, but argue that national resources now devoted to drug law enforcement could be better spent on demand reduction. Although the media have given considerable attention to the proposal, legalization has not received any significant political support. Recent polls indicate that more than 80 percent of Americans oppose legalization, and two-thirds believe that marijuana possession should be a criminal offense.

There are, of course, other policy alternatives. Some experts contend that while all illicit drugs are dangerous, their consequences differ both in severity and impact. Some argue that crack, for example, which is highly addictive and produces violent behavior, presents a more immediate threat to individuals and society than does marijuana, which is dangerous but not as destructive. Advocates of intermediate policies would maintain the present drug laws but would channel limited resources to substances that present the greatest threat rather than use them indiscriminately to combat all drugs.

Federal Drug Control Strategy between 1968 and 1981

Declaring war on drug abuse shortly after taking office in 1969, President Nixon changed the emphasis on law enforcement to make demand reduction his primary focus. He created the Special Action Office of Drug Abuse Prevention (SAODAP) in 1971. Headed by a director authorized to supervise all federal drug abuse prevention, treatment, rehabilitation, and research programs, SAODAP was housed in its own building across the street from the White House. The president often participated in meetings of the Strategy Council on Drug Abuse. In 1972, Congress formally established SAODAP for a three-year period.

From 1970 to 1975, prevention, education, and treatment programs received almost two-thirds of the total drug budget—$1.92 billion out of $3 billion. From 1976 to 1981, demand reduction received about 43 percent of the total $5.2 billion drug budget. In 1982, the first full funding year under the Reagan administration, a radical shift occurred: of the $1.3 billion drug budget, law enforcement received almost 80 percent of the total, relegating demand reduction to a much smaller role. This pattern of funding continued until Congress passed the Anti-Drug Abuse Act of 1988.

Considerable continuity in federal drug policy existed during the administrations of Presidents Nixon, Ford, and Carter. All gave priority to curtailing the use of heroin, targeting traffickers rather than users, and providing treatment for drug abusers. The implicit objective was to contain rather than cure the drug problem.

Supply control efforts were important in the 1960s and 1970s but not nearly as important as they became in the 1980s. International efforts to reduce the supply of drugs coming into the United States were given high priority.

Beginning with President Nixon's Operation Intercept in 1969, which effectively closed a key point on the U.S.-Mexican border for three weeks in response to Mexican marijuana and heroin production, international cooperation played a critical role in supply reduction. Similarly, during the 1970s, cooperative programs with Turkey and Mexico reduced the heroin coming into the United States.

The theory behind the reduction of international supplies, particularly heroin, is that the resulting shortages within the United States would reinforce domestic demand reduction efforts. Reduced supplies mean higher prices, causing some abusers to stop or to seek treatment. Increased prices may also deter potential new users, particularly teenagers, from trying the drug. Even short-term reductions in supply can create a window of opportunity for treatment and prevention efforts.

MAJOR SHIFTS IN STRATEGY: 1981–1988

The Reagan administration substantially changed the focus of U.S. drug policy while appearing to maintain the overall direction set by earlier administrations. Supply reduction efforts continued, as did the public rhetoric about waging an all-out war on drugs; in fact, the emphasis shifted increasingly to border interdiction. Further, the Reagan administration differed fundamentally from its predecessors by downplaying the importance of demand reduction in controlling drug abuse. It also placed less importance on international efforts to reduce the production of illicit drugs grown for the American market.

Concentration on Drug Law Enforcement

The single most significant change that the Reagan administration made in drug policy was to consider drug abuse almost exclusively a problem of law enforcement.

Figure 3.1

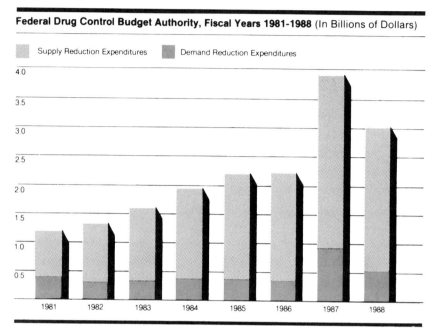

Federal Drug Control Budget Authority, Fiscal Years 1981-1988 (In Billions of Dollars)

Supply Reduction Expenditures   Demand Reduction Expenditures

Note: 1987 and 1988 figures are as estimated in the President's 1988 Budget.

Source: National Drug Enforcement Policy Board.

Based on the assumption that abuse, particularly among young people, reflected an overly tolerant approach by earlier administrations, President Reagan believed the key to changing that behavior was tougher enforcement of the drug laws and expanded interdiction efforts.

In the first year of the new administration, federal spending for drug-related law enforcement programs, including interdiction, investigations, and prosecutions, jumped 50 percent. From 1981 through 1986, funding for law enforcement more than doubled—from $800 million in 1981 to $1.9 billion in 1986 (see Figure 3.1). About 90 percent of the total increase in federal drug control funding from 1981 to 1986 went to law enforcement. Attorney General Edwin Meese, head of the national Drug Policy Board, noted in 1987 that these had been "the largest increases in drug law enforcement funding and manpower in the nation's history."

Reduced Support for Demand Reduction

While doubling support for drug law enforcement, the Reagan administration made substantial cuts in demand reduction programs. Total federal funding for prevention, education, and treatment declined from $404 million in 1981 to $338 million in 1985; when adjusted for inflation, this amounted to a reduction of almost 40 percent. Drug abuse prevention and education programs received an average of $23 million a year during the same period.

These cuts in demand reduction programs undermined the basic premise of earlier U.S. drug policy: that a reduction in illicit supplies would force addicts into treatment and prevent potential new users from trying drugs. The Reagan policy no longer linked supply reduction directly to demand reduction because treatment was often unavailable for addicts who could not afford private care.

The Reagan administration also weakened federal leadership in demand reduction programs by shifting funding to the states through block grants. Instead of using federally administered categorical grants, beginning in 1982, funds were distributed directly to the states in block grants for alcohol, drug abuse, and mental health services. States were given wide discretion to establish programs within broadly defined areas. Previously, through the categorical grant system, which provided funds for specific programs that met federal guidelines, NIDA had set the direction of prevention and treatment programs since its creation in 1973. When the block grant system was instituted, NIDA became essentially a research agency without operating responsibility in the drug field.

Increased Emphasis on Border Interdiction

An early policy initiative of the Reagan administration was to improve border interdiction, particularly at key entry points like southern Florida, by increasing both resources and interagency cooperation. Vice President George Bush chaired the South Florida Task Force of the National Narcotic Border Interdiction System, which included hundreds of officials detailed from the U.S. Customs Service, the Coast Guard, the Drug Enforcement Administration (DEA), and the Justice and Treasury departments.

Although the task force received considerable publicity when it was created in 1982, its efforts did not lead to a decrease in drugs coming into the country. A review of interdiction efforts by the U.S. General Accounting Office (GAO) in 1983 found that more drugs were entering the United States than five years earlier, and that only 10 percent were being intercepted. In 1985, another GAO study reported similarly discouraging results. Nevertheless, funds for drug interdiction more than doubled from $263 million in 1981 to $605 million in 1986. Interdiction now represents 38 percent of the federal drug enforcement program.[3]

THE FAILURE OF THE 1981-1988 FEDERAL DRUG STRATEGY

By 1986, top administration officials acknowledged publicly that their drug control strategy had failed. The failure was due to an overreliance on drug law enforcement at the expense of both demand reduction and international efforts. President Reagan admitted in a major speech before the 1986 elections that "all the confiscation and law enforcement in the world will not cure this plague." The failure also arose because the administration did not respond to rapidly changing patterns of illicit drug production and abuse, notably crack, or to the AIDS crisis, which was closely linked to intravenous drug use.

Overreliance on Drug Law Enforcement

The success of drug law enforcement efforts in reducing illicit drug supplies has traditionally been measured by increases in drug price and decreases in purity. These adjustments reflect the additional costs the traffickers must bear as a result of tougher interdiction, larger seizures, and more arrests. The traffickers generally pass such cost increases along to the consumer. By these measures of price and purity, the Reagan administration's drug control strategy was a failure from the beginning.

In 1981, a kilogram of cocaine sold wholesale in Miami for $60,000. By 1983, the kilogram price had dropped by half, and the downward slide has continued. In 1987, the National Narcotics Intelligence Consumers Committee (NNICC) found that "cocaine wholesale prices during the year were the lowest ever reported, and the purity remained at high levels, reflecting widespread availability." Today, a kilogram of cocaine sells wholesale for as little as $10,000. Heroin and marijuana availability and potency also increased.

Increased competition from U.S. growers between 1981 and 1985 was a key factor in the wholesale price drop of marijuana coming from other countries. Many foreign traffickers thus turned to cocaine, a much more difficult target of interdiction than the bulkier marijuana. Drug enforcement officials estimate that a single cargo plane fully loaded with cocaine could supply the nation's current demand for a year.

Illicit coca production in Peru and Bolivia quickly expanded to supply the new cocaine trafficking networks, and prices fell dramatically at every level. This precipitous drop set the stage for the development of crack, a breakthrough that both multiplied cocaine profits for street-level dealers and created a new group of addicts. Because crack can be produced cheaply and easily from cocaine and can be sold in much cheaper units, it is far more profitable than cocaine for the pusher. For example, one ounce of cocaine, which costs about $1,600, can be converted into 400 vials of crack, which sell for $4,000 or more.[4] This profit margin greatly expanded the number of low-level street dealers, especially young people who had not previously been part of the drug traffic.

Inadequate International Efforts

Despite the rhetorical importance placed on diplomatic initiatives, the Reagan administration did not rely on international efforts to reduce illicit drug supplies coming into the United States. Faced with explosive increases in coca production in South America in the early 1980s, the administration did not launch major international supply control programs. While coca production more than doubled between 1981 and 1986, the administration's international narcotics control program received an average of $43 million a year, only slightly more than the funding levels of the mid-1970s, when the international program accounted for about 10 percent of the total supply reduction effort. By 1986, it represented only 3 percent of total drug law enforcement funding, which had more than doubled since the beginning of the decade.

Not only was the Reagan administration slow to respond to the explosion of South American coca production; it continued to rely on the policy models developed for cooperation with Turkey and Mexico in the 1970s. Those models reflected clear national interests on both sides: both governments agreed to strong narcotics control actions in return for a major commitment of U.S. resources—$35 million for Turkey's income-substitution program in the early 1970s and $100 million for Mexico's aerial eradication campaign in the late 1970s. (See appendixes to this chapter for more information on U.S. collaboration with Turkey and Mexico and for a brief look at the United Nations drug control effort.)

The success of those arrangements depended on several key elements: a strong central government with political control over the countryside; active commitment by the government to undertake often unpopular drug control measures; effective techniques for eradicating production. None of these factors was characteristic of the South American producing countries. A particularly critical obstacle was the failure to find a relatively safe herbicide to destroy coca. As a result, coca production expanded virtually unchecked, and the Reagan administration made little effort to help the producing countries develop effective new policies to counter this radically different and much more dangerous increase in illicit drug production.

Lack of Leadership

The rapid increase in federal funding for drug law enforcement in the early 1980s compounded existing problems of coordination among the dozens of federal agencies responsible for the drug effort. In the absence of clear policy direction, agencies engaged in open competition for resources and authority. The struggle between the Coast Guard and the Customs Service for control of interdiction was often cited in the press, especially when both agencies took credit for the same drug seizure. In response to the mounting bureaucratic confusion, Congress passed a bill in 1983 to place central responsibility for all aspects of the federal drug control program—law enforcement, education, prevention, treatment, and international operations—in one cabinet-level official. President Reagan vetoed the legislation, despite its strong bipartisan support, ostensibly on the grounds that it was not necessary to have another cabinet-level position. The real reason seemed to be that Attorney General Edwin Meese, who headed the National Drug Policy Board, did not want to cede the Justice Department's leadership role. Despite con-

tinuing opposition from President Reagan, Congress created the "drug czar," the director of the new Office of National Drug Policy Control, as part of the Anti-Drug Abuse
Act of 1988.

CONSEQUENCES OF THE FOCUS
ON LAW ENFORCEMENT

At the heart of the failure of federal drug strategy under
the Reagan administration was the decision to separate
law enforcement from prevention and treatment. Enforcement virtually became an end in itself, its success measured in terms of increased drug arrests, seizures, and
criminal convictions. This led to intolerable strains on the
criminal justice system and severe prison overcrowding without producing any reductions in drug abuse and
crime.

What the Reagan administration failed to appreciate
was the relative inelasticity of the demand for drugs
among addicts. Tightening enforcement without at the
same time providing treatment leads to increased crime
by addicts trying to obtain money. Even crack, which is
relatively inexpensive in small, individual doses, is so
highly addictive that chronic use quickly becomes costly
to maintain.

By 1987, NIDA estimated that publicly funded treatment was available for less than 4 percent of the estimated 6.5 million drug users/addicts in need of help.
Methadone maintenance programs in New York City can
accommodate only 30,000 of the city's estimated 200,000
heroin addicts. Only a few prisons have drug programs to
treat the increasingly large numbers of drug-dependent
offenders. The reduction of drug treatment resources at
a time of intensified enforcement had a devastating effect
on poor neighborhoods, which were particularly vulnera-
ble to rapid increases in addiction and violent crime. The

spread of AIDS by intravenous drug users also went unchecked because of lack of treatment opportunities.

Tighter drug law enforcement sought to discourage drug
experimentation by new users, particularly young people,
by driving up prices and instilling a fear of getting caught.
Prevention and education programs for youngsters were
designed to teach them to recognize and resist drugs. Yet,
despite frequent speeches by President and Mrs. Reagan
on the importance of prevention, the administration gave
virtually no financial support to these efforts. From 1982
through 1985, prevention and education received about
$23 million a year, only 1 percent of total drug abuse fund-
ing.[5] By relegating demand reduction to a minor role, the
administration also lost valuable time in meeting the
challenges posed by expanding cocaine and crack use. New
models of prevention and treatment were urgently needed; however, without federal policy leadership and financial support, little progress was made.

THE CONGRESSIONAL RESPONSE

By 1986, both the administration and Congress recognized
that the massive emphasis on supply control was not suc-
ceeding. Widespread concern over the failure of drug policy led Congress to adopt a comprehensive Anti-Drug Abuse
Act in October 1986, which provided more than $1.7 bil-
lion in new funds. Combined with previously existing federal drug programs, overall funding climbed to $3.9 billion.

The act more than doubled money available for demand
reduction activities, from $400 million in 1986 to $950 million in 1987. It also provided a tenfold increase for prevention and education activities, jumping from about $24
million in 1986 to $249 million in 1987. A major portion
of this new money—$200 million in 1987 and $250 million 1988 and 1989—was authorized for block grants
through the Department of Education for drug abuse

Figure 3.2

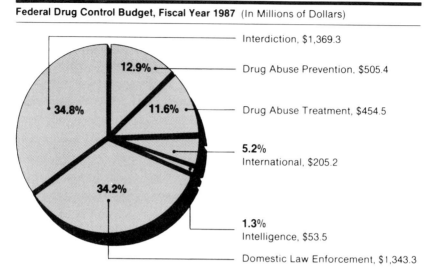

Federal Drug Control Budget, Fiscal Year 1987 (In Millions of Dollars)

- Interdiction, $1,369.3
- Drug Abuse Prevention, $505.4
- Drug Abuse Treatment, $454.5
- International, $205.2
- Intelligence, $53.5
- Domestic Law Enforcement, $1,343.3

Note 1: Domestic Law Enforcement includes investigation, prosecution, and diversion control.

Note 2: Total Budget Authority is $3.9 billion.

Source: National Drug Enforcement Policy Board.

prevention and education. Even with this increased attention to demand reduction, however, supply reduction continued to receive more than three-quarters of the total $3.9 billion authorized (see Figure 3.2).

President Reagan publicly praised the new legislation and declared a "national crusade" against drugs. But two months after the congressional elections of November 1986, in which drug abuse had been a major campaign issue, the administration quietly tried to cut 60 percent from drug prevention and education funds and eliminate any new money for drug treatment programs as well as state and local law enforcement support. Overriding the president's action, Congress was able to restore most of the funds.

Public frustration with the continuing failure of federal drug control policy and the heavy reliance on law enforcement as the primary strategy led Congress to adopt a new Anti-Drug Abuse Act in 1988. The Senate version of the bill would have mandated that 55 percent of the appropriations be allocated to demand reduction, but in the House-Senate conference, specific percentage allocations were dropped.

The 1988 act authorized $2.75 billion in new money in addition to the president's budget request of $3.9 billion. However, in order to remain within the deficit ceiling, only $500 million of the new funds can be spent in 1989; almost half will support demand reduction programs.[6]

In addition to increasing the importance of demand reduction, the new act establishes tougher penalties for traffickers, including the death penalty for dealers who murder in the course of their dealing as well as for anyone who kills a police officer during drug trafficking activities. The act also establishes new "user accountability" provisions aimed at so-called middle-class users. Those found with small amounts of drugs for personal use can now be assessed civil fines up to $10,000, while courts are given discretion to deny federal benefits, such as school and housing loans, to convicted dealers and users.

The original House bill contained tougher penalties as well as changes in the exclusionary rules governing admissible evidence. The modifications were part of a last-minute compromise between House and Senate leaders before the 1988 adjournment.

APPENDIX 1

U.S. Collaboration with Turkey and Mexico

Turkey became the primary source of opium for heroin coming into the United States in the mid-1960s—the first link of the famous "French Connection." At the time, opium was legal in Turkey; the opium poppy had long been an important agricultural crop. It provided cooking oil, fuel, and seeds, in addition to being exported for medicinal manufacture of codeine and morphine. As worldwide demand for heroin increased in the 1960s, traffickers began buying Turkish opium for heroin refineries in France and Sicily.

The American public reacted strongly to the increase in heroin imports. Political pressure mounted to cut off the supply of opium from Turkey and to break the French trafficking connection. In response to U.S. threats to cut off all foreign assistance, the Turkish government banned opium production in 1972. Alternative means of livelihood were found for many of the opium growers with UN and U.S. assistance. At the same time, the United States worked closely with the French government to bring about the arrest of the major traffickers who had been operating heroin refining labs in Marseilles and shipping heroin from France to the United States.

By 1974, internal domestic pressure caused the Turkish government to reinstate limited opium production in strictly controlled areas monitored by the United Nations. Today, Turkey and India are the only licensed suppliers of opiates for U.S. pharmaceutical needs. Neither country has become a source for the international heroin market.

When the Turkish-French connection was broken in 1972, with an abrupt interruption in heroin supplies, international traffickers turned to Mexico. Mexico's proximity to the United States gave the traffickers an immediate advantage over the distant routes from Southeast Asia, the other major source of heroin. By 1975, Mexico supplied 87 percent of the heroin in the United States (and 95 percent of the marijuana).

Again in response to U.S. pressure, as well as internal political concerns, the Mexican government undertook a massive herbicidal eradication campaign in 1976 to destroy opium and marijuana cultivation. More than $100 million in U.S. assistance from 1976 to 1981 enabled the eradication campaign to employ the most modern technology available. The impact was dramatic: by 1980, the Mexican share of the U.S. heroin market dropped to 25 percent; marijuana supplies dropped to 10 percent.[1]

Since 1985, however, Mexico has reemerged as the primary supplier of heroin and marijuana to the United States, as well as a major transit point for cocaine produced in South America. This happened for a variety of reasons, including the sharp drop in oil prices, which drastically reduced Mexican hard currency earnings. Political relations with the United States were also strained, stemming from high-level criticism of Mexico by the U.S. government, particularly in relation to the 1985 murder of DEA agent Enrique Camarena. Recently, cooperation has improved, as the new administration of President Carlos Salinas de Gortari strengthened drug enforcement and arrested several major traffickers, and as the Bush administration indicated its eagerness to find ways to reduce Mexico's heavy burden of external debt service.

An unintended, paradoxical result of Mexico's success in reducing marijuana production in the 1970s was to stimulate illicit production in the United States. In 1976, when Mexico began the eradication campaign, Mexican marijuana was relatively cheap ($25 per ounce) and of low potency (1 percent THC content). Spraying the herbicide paraquat on most marijuana fields eliminated much of the crop, but that which survived continued to come into the United States and raised widespread concern about adverse health effects on marijuana users. As a result, Mexican imports plummeted.

Jamaica and Colombia, until then two relatively minor marijuana suppliers for the U.S. markets, quickly stepped up production to meet demand. Their product was both

more potent and more expensive than the Mexican variety, increasing health hazards for users as well as profits
for traffickers. At the same time, illicit production in the
United States continued to expand. By the early 1980s,
marijuana had become the largest cash crop in California, Hawaii, and Oregon. Assessing the impact of the
marijuana eradication and interdiction campaign, a recent
Rand study observed that "it may turn out, unfortunate-
ly, that the United States has at last managed (rather ex-
pensively) to provide effective tariff protection for one
industry: marijuana production."[2] By 1987, the NNICC estimated that domestic marijuana production supplied 25
percent of the U.S. market.

For heroin, if measured solely in terms of availability,
U.S. drug policy during the 1970s was relatively successful. After the Turkish ban on opium cultivation in 1972,
supplies dropped significantly and brought about a reduction in American heroin addiction for several years.
However, as Mexican heroin production expanded in the
mid-1970s, the price declined, use increased, and by 1976,
there were an estimated 550,000 addicts.

By 1979, as the effects of the Mexican eradication campaign were felt, heroin again became less available in the
United States. Prices increased, the purity of the street
drug decreased, and the number of heroin addicts declined
to an estimated 450,000.

APPENDIX 2

United Nations and Regional Organizations

United Nations drug control agencies have played an increasingly important role as drug abuse problems in both
consumer and producer countries have proliferated. The
International Narcotics Control Board (INCB) issues an
annual report on worldwide production and use of illicit

drugs and oversees compliance with the two major multilateral drug control treaties, the 1961 Single Convention on Narcotic Drugs and the 1971 Convention on Psychotropic Substances.

The Commission on Narcotic Drugs (CND) is responsible for formulating international drug control policy and recently adopted a new convention on drug trafficking. When ratified by twenty nations, it will require all signatory governments to enact laws permitting extradition of suspected traffickers and seizure of their bank accounts and property. It will preclude member nations from invoking secrecy laws to block investigations into the assets of international drug syndicates, and it will include the right to board and search vessels of another country suspected of running drugs.

The United Nations Fund for Drug Abuse Control (UNFDAC) was established in 1971 to coordinate multilateral programs to control drug production, trafficking, and abuse. U.S. support for UNFDAC remained essentially constant at about $3.2 million a year from 1981 through 1986. In 1987, a contribution of $5 million by the U.S. Agency for International Development (AID) for development programs in opium-growing areas of Pakistan brought the U.S. total to $8.8 million, its largest to date. In 1989, the contribution dropped to $1 million. Compared to other industrialized countries, the U.S. contributions have not been great. U.S. support for a number of other regional organizations to combat drug abuse has also been very limited, totaling less than $300,000 a year.

Chapter 4

Demand Reduction— What Works?

The failure of drug law enforcement as the dominant strategy to combat drug abuse has recently led to a rediscovery of the strategy of demand reduction. Starting in 1986, President Reagan, Attorney General Meese, and other top law enforcement officials began to acknowledge that drug abuse prevention, education, and treatment might work better than supply reduction. However, because these programs had been neglected since 1981, few effective models existed for present patterns of drug abuse, particularly crack. Nevertheless, a number of recent initiatives urgently deserve further study.

PREVENTION

Primary prevention—stopping use before it begins as well as preventing experimental use from becoming abuse—clearly seems the most effective way to reduce demand. However, only fragmentary research has been done on the long-term impact of prevention campaigns on individual behavior. What is known is that most previous drug abuse prevention efforts in the United States were not successful. In fact, some of these programs may have actually increased experimentation with drugs.

The earliest prevention efforts at the beginning of the century were moral exhortations advocating temperance or abstinence from alcohol and drugs—not unlike the "Just Say No" campaign of the 1980s. When this approach did not work, Congress decided to ban the substances, believing that supply control would succeed where demand reduction had failed. Although the constitutional amendment prohibiting alcohol enacted in 1919 was repealed in 1933, the prohibition of other drugs, like heroin, has remained in effect since the Harrison Narcotic Act of 1914.

After exhortations, the second major prevention technique was scare tactics. A good example is the short film *Reefer Madness,* produced in 1937, the year marijuana was outlawed. The film became a cult classic among the generation of young marijuana users of the late 1960s. It depicted the precipitous downfall of a promising young man who tried one puff of a marijuana cigarette, or "reefer." But since many young people found that terrible things did not occur when they tried marijuana, they stopped believing all negative drug information. The resulting loss of adult credibility set back efforts to influence the burgeoning numbers of adolescent drug users.

More recent approaches to drug education focused on information—specifically, on providing data about the negative pharmacologic, legal, and health consequences of drug use. However, analyses of these programs found that they often aroused some interest in trying drugs, perhaps because a drug's mood-altering effects were presented as well as its dangers. The studies also showed that information alone is not sufficient to change either attitudes or behavior toward drug use.

The next development in drug-prevention efforts was "affective" education—a strategy to foster self-esteem and improve social skills and problem-solving abilities, often without specific reference to drugs. This model of education assumes that young people use drugs to compensate for inadequacies in other areas, but it ignores the pleasure and relief from stress that many young people find in drugs. There was little emphasis on the real-life skills that students need to cope with the various internal and external pressures to use alcohol and drugs. A purely rational or psychological understanding of the costs and benefits of drug use has not been shown to affect subsequent use.[1] Despite their apparent lack of effectiveness, however, variants of these programs have been used in many schools since the mid-1970s.

New School-based Prevention Initiatives

The psychosocial factors involved in the initiation of substance use are the focus of promising new approaches to prevention. The premise is that individuals create their environment by choosing social situations and friends, and that tobacco, alcohol, and drug use is a learned reaction to environmental and personal factors.[2] The emphasis and implementation of these programs vary. Some build students' awareness of the pressures to smoke and teach them specific techniques for resisting them; others emphasize the general development of individual competence. All attempt to reduce the motivation to smoke and to teach children how to function more competently in challenging social situations.

The success of these new prevention programs appears to be greater than with earlier techniques and may be relevant to drug and alcohol prevention.[3] Primary prevention of smoking may discourage young people from trying other drugs, since tobacco, along with alcohol, is considered a "gateway" drug leading to marijuana and often to "harder" drugs like cocaine and heroin.[4]

These new prevention programs are now being tested in schools around the country. Until very recently, most of the programs were directed toward white, middle-class schoolchildren. Many adolescents at greatest risk have dropped out of school, but efforts are beginning to reach those who remain in classrooms.[5]

Many states suffered from the drastically reduced federal support for prevention efforts from 1981 to 1987. In Oregon, for example, only 5 percent of the total drug budget went for prevention during this period, since the funds were critically needed for treatment. Some school districts with teachers who are already overburdened have been reluctant to introduce new prevention programs, which can be costly to implement, particularly since their effectiveness has not yet been proven.

Community-based Prevention Programs

In addition to school-based prevention programs, organized parent groups—now estimated to exceed 7,000—have proliferated in response to growing concerns about adolescent drug use. These community efforts generally attempt to establish "zero tolerance" for any alcohol or drug use; they aim to teach children to "just say no."[6]

The growth of these local groups is one reflection of parental frustration at the lack of government leadership in drug prevention. Most of these efforts are organized by middle-class parents against marijuana and alcohol use by their children. Rates of experimentation are high among this group, but the frequency of serious drug problems is relatively low.

Minority, inner-city children, who are at highest risk for drug abuse, are generally not reached by prevention efforts. A major three-year project sponsored by the Robert Wood Johnson Foundation sought to provide health care, including help with drug and alcohol problems, for teenagers in more than a dozen cities. When the project was unable to attract many young people, it was redesigned to operate in high schools, where it reaches greater numbers of students but often not those at highest risk. In the 1986 Anti-Drug Abuse Act, Congress created a special grant program to develop new prevention models for this group.

Media Campaigns

The role of the media in influencing drug use is significant. Television especially helps create and reflect the values that shape perceptions of acceptable social behavior. Ads for alcohol and tobacco were found to have such a powerful impact that, except for beer and wine, they can no longer be shown on television. Similarly, the reduction in smoking during the late 1970s may have been helped by the antismoking spots. Between 1977 and 1981, the proportion of high school seniors who smoked daily decreased by one-third. The perceived harmfulness of smoking rose with each successive senior class through 1980, suggesting their attitudes were influenced by the negative publicity on smoking. Some researchers believe that the antismoking bias may have had a spillover effect in discouraging marijuana smoking, which began to decline in 1980.

Recent public service announcements use well-known sports, media, and rock figures who have recovered from drug abuse to urge children not to follow their example. Some experts believe that the message is ambiguous: The role model is admired, and he has used drugs. As a result, drugs themselves are not necessarily "deglamorized."

An entirely new approach was started in 1986 by the Partnership for a Drug-Free America, a volunteer nationwide coalition of major advertising, media, and public communications firms. The Partnership's goal is to "unsell" illegal drugs and encourage hostile attitudes toward drug consumption in an attempt to reverse the positive perception of marijuana, cocaine, and crack held by one out of seven teenagers.[7] The ads also try to dispel the notion, held by more than a third of children ages 9–12, that drug users are popular.

This is the largest and most sophisticated antidrug media campaign ever undertaken. A base study measuring public attitudes toward drugs before the ads were aired was conducted in February 1987. A follow-up study was done a year later. Among all age groups, attitudes toward drug use had become more negative, particularly among college students and children and in areas with high media coverage of the ads. In addition, college students reported significant declines in cocaine use. The Partnership plans to conduct annual tracking studies on the effects of the campaign, at the same time gathering data on public attitudes not previously collected by the NIDA-sponsored national surveys.

A recent media campaign by the Harvard University School of Public Health has been designed to change social norms about the acceptability of driving after drinking. The theory behind this effort, like the Partnership campaign, is that the media can influence community values and thus significantly mold individual behavior.

In summary, both the development and the evaluation of promising prevention models are in the earliest stages. However, the challenge of reaching the highest-risk adolescents, particularly inner-city minorities, has not yet been adequately addressed. For them, the research is only now beginning.

TREATMENT

Major cuts in federal funding since 1981 have meant limited availability of drug treatment for most users. There are an estimated 1.3 million intravenous drug users in the United States; publicly funded programs treat 148,000 at a time. In many cities, waiting periods for admission to treatment programs are six months or more.

Public concern about the rapid spread of AIDS by intravenous drug users has recently led to increased support for treatment programs. The report of the Presidential Commission on AIDS in June 1988 strongly recommended expanded drug treatment—$15 billion over the next decade—as the most cost-effective way to contain the AIDS epidemic. The report pointed out that treating the effects of AIDS often costs more than $100,000 per person. The yearly costs of drug treatment range from $2,300 a person for drug-free outpatient programs to $3,000 each for methadone maintenance programs. (Residential programs that keep addicts in treatment for eighteen months or longer cost as much as $14,600 a year.)[8]

Types of Treatment Programs

Most treatment programs begin with detoxification, the medically supervised withdrawal from the drug on which the person has become dependent. Although it is generally the first step in a long-term treatment program, detoxification itself provides important benefits by breaking the cycle of addiction. A 1982 study of detoxified heroin addicts found that daily drug use declined by as much as one-third the following year.[9]

Methadone is a synthetic drug that is administered orally to relieve the craving for heroin. Introduced in the 1960s, methadone is used to maintain addicts as a substitute for heroin.[10]

Drug-free, residential treatment programs attempt to change addictive behavior through a highly structured approach. Often using former addicts as counselors, the programs generally emphasize self-help and individual responsibility, working in group therapy sessions that stress honesty and openness. Dropout rates are high: a survey of seven programs in 1984 found that retention rates for a year ranged from 4 to 21 percent.[11] Patients who remain at least three months show positive results in reduced drug use and criminality and increased employment. Those who stay for a year or longer show substantially greater improvement in all areas.[12]

Drug-free, nonresidential treatment programs include a wide variety of approaches, ranging from drop-in activity centers to highly structured counseling. They account for nearly half of all patients in treatment. Among the most effective programs are those based on the Alcoholics Anonymous model that provide strong group support for addicts and their families (Cocaine Anonymous,[13] Narcotics Anonymous, and Co-Anon, for example) and treat drug abuse as a continuing, chronic disease. These groups are run free of charge by volunteers who have had drug and alcohol problems; members often join them after completing residential or other outpatient treatment.

Recent research confirms that all drug treatment lowers use and crime among the patient population for at least some period of time. After that, family problems, employment skills, and psychiatric problems determine the relative effectiveness of various treatment approaches. Classifying patients according to a "problem severity profile," a major study of drug treatment found that low-severity patients (approximately 15 percent; those without psychiatric problems) did extremely well in all types of treatment programs and showed the highest level of improvement. High-severity patients (20 percent, who have serious depression and anxiety) did very poorly, regardless of the type of program. The mid-severity group (65 percent of the total, with moderate symptoms of anxiety and depression) showed a range of outcomes depending on the type of program. For them, matching types of patients with specific programs was shown to improve outcomes.[14]

Treatment methods for cocaine and crack addiction are still in the early stages of formulation. Severe depressive symptoms after cocaine withdrawal make program participation difficult; however, some clinicians have reported that acupuncture treatment as well as antidepressant drugs like desipramine decrease cocaine craving. Crack addicts are harder to treat than any other drug abusers, in part because the drug is so rapidly addictive. Researchers estimate that less than a quarter of crack addicts remain drug-free for six months in most treatment programs.[15]

Because of a lack of resources, programs to treat crack addiction have been slow in developing. Highly structured programs with intensive follow-up care seem to produce the best results. Phoenix House in New York City reports that half of those admitted drop out. Those who stay at least six months have a 70 percent likelihood of staying off crack at least a year after they leave the program. While follow-up support groups like Cocaine Anonymous are particularly important, researchers fear that crack addiction may not be curable; it may be (even more than other types of addiction) a chronic disease in which relapse is frequent. New treatment models will have to take that possibility into account.

Adolescent Drug Treatment

There is no reliable current information on young people receiving treatment for drug problems. The last available nationwide figures are from 1981, when NIDA estimated that 12 percent of the total treatment population was under 18, and most were in treatment for marijuana, cocaine, and alcohol abuse; only 1.5 percent were being treated for heroin addiction. The rising trend of cocaine abuse was already apparent: the percentage of adolescents in treatment for cocaine abuse rose from 1.1 percent in 1978 to 4.1 percent in 1981.[16]

Little work has been done on designing treatment programs specifically for adolescents.[17] Instead, youths generally have gone into adult programs that often do not consider the unique problems of adolescent drug abusers and the importance of their family situations.

There is little systematic data on the effectiveness of
adolescent treatment, but what there is shows that
teenagers who remain in residential drug treatment programs three months or longer reduce their alcohol and
drug use, while those in outpatient programs have generally not done as well.[18]

Private Treatment Programs

In recent years there has been rapid growth of private,
residential treatment programs operated by for-profit cor-
porations. Laws in twenty-four states now require
employer-sponsored benefits for substance abuse treatment. As a result, many acute-care general hospitals seeking to improve low occupancy rates have converted
inpatient beds to special drug treatment programs.[19] Many
of these private programs operate on a mental health
residential program model that uses psychiatrically
trained staff, rather than on the therapeutic community
model, which relies on peer influence and group action to
change behavior.

Because of the high cost of treatment in private facilities, many companies have placed limits on drug treatment
benefits. The 1987 Foster Higgins Health Care Benefits
Survey found that three-quarters of the 2,000 employers
surveyed limit the number of inpatient days an employee
can spend in treatment each year, the maximum dollar
amount payable for treatment claims, and the number of
lifetime drug abuse hospitalizations per patient. Some
companies are attempting to exclude health coverage for
diseases brought on by "life-style" choices, notably AIDS
and drug abuse.[20]

DRUG TESTING

As a new form of demand reduction, drug testing has become widespread for employees in the private sector as well

as in government.[21] Testing is seen both by business and government as a deterrent as well as a device to contain the costs stemming from drug abuse, lost productivity, absenteeism, and illness. Testing is also viewed as a means to reduce the risk of accidents, particularly in safety-sensitive jobs.

Increasing numbers of businesses require pre-employment drug testing. The 1988 Bureau of Labor Statistics survey found that 3.9 million job applicants had been tested during the previous year, of which 11.9 percent tested positive. Some companies, such as IBM, test all applicants. Those who test positive are informed immediately and allowed to reapply for employment in six months. A second positive test, however, bars them from further reapplication.

Highly accurate tests are available to detect the presence of drug metabolites in urine. Despite the reliability of the technology, though, careless or negligent laboratory work can lead to inaccurate results. The U.S. Navy had to reverse all positive findings for certain drug tests in 1981, and rehire the people fired as a result of sloppy lab work. New federal guidelines require certification of drug-testing facilities by NIDA and impose tough quality controls and frequent inspections of laboratories.

Even when drug tests are accurate, they provide only limited information. Marijuana metabolites may be present in the urine for seven days, while cocaine and amphetamines are difficult to detect more than forty-eight hours after use. Opiates can be traced two to four days after use. Drug tests do not reveal, however, whether the person is an occasional user or a chronic abuser, or the degree of impairment caused by drug use.

Federal guidelines require government agencies to offer drug treatment to those who test positive, but leave it to the agency's discretion whether or not to institute disciplinary action.

Drug testing used for deterrent purposes is limited by

the information provided by urinalysis, which is only valid within a week of the test. Only continuous, random drug testing would identify the regular, controlled user, who can suspend drug use well before a scheduled test. Advocates of testing nonetheless believe it helps identify those who might cause workplace problems or endanger the public safety. The potential loss of employment, they argue, can be a powerful motive for changing behavior.

The deterrent function of testing is seen most clearly with criminal offenders. Urinalysis is used in increasing numbers of jurisdictions to help determine eligibility for pretrial release and parole. Once an offender is released, testing positive for drugs results in immediate incarceration. Proponents also believe that testing improves the efficiency of the criminal justice system in deciding which offenders are most likely to commit crimes. Studies by the National Institute of Justice indicate that drug users are much more likely to commit serious offenses than nonusers.[22] The studies also show that those who have been arrested and use drugs while on pretrial release commit twice as much crime as those who remain drug-free.

Mandatory drug testing has been widely challenged as violating the Fourth Amendment of the Constitution, which protects the individual against unreasonable search and seizure. Although courts have generally held that mandatory testing does constitute search and seizure within the meaning of the Fourth Amendment, they have disagreed on whether the testing is unreasonable. In March 1989, the Supreme Court upheld drug-testing programs begun by the Reagan administration for the railroad industry and, in most respects, for U.S. Customs Service agents. The Court gave the federal government broad discretion to test employees where duties involve public safety or law enforcement. However, the Court did not clearly define the permissible limits of testing, so that further litigation will be necessary to clarify the future parameters of government testing programs.

Chapter 5

A Proposed National Drug Strategy

The nation's war against drugs requires a long-term commitment of political will and resources that is not dependent on the vagaries of the election cycle. It must be based on strategies that reflect the most informed thinking about what works.

The failure of drug policy during this decade has taught us what does not work, particularly the dangers of overreliance on a single response to the complexities of drug abuse. Like the nation's commitment to finding a cure for cancer, the nation's drug strategy should seek to contain the spread of drugs through a variety of approaches (law enforcement, international cooperation, prevention, and treatment) while continuing the long-term search for primary prevention and effective treatment.

The war on drugs will require strong leadership and broad public support. A new strategy should therefore provide an opportunity for public debate on what the goals of national drug policy should be, taking into account the severe budgetary constraints imposed by the Gramm-Rudman-Hollings Budget Deficit Act, which at present permits spending only a fifth of the total funds authorized in 1989. Unless Congress finds new sources of funding, hard choices will have to be made among competing priorities.

RECOMMENDATIONS

The recommendations that follow do not address the structural problems of poverty and race that are clearly tied to problems of drug abuse and trafficking. No drug policy, however effective, can by itself address the deepening crisis of the nation's inner cities; other private and public programs will have to provide real opportunities in employment, housing, and education. Drug policies can, however, reduce the damage that drug abuse inflicts on millions of Americans through prevention, enforcement, and treatment programs.

A. DRUG LAW ENFORCEMENT

1. Target Resources against the Most Dangerous Drugs

The federal government should concentrate its limited law enforcement resources on combating the most dangerous drugs, namely heroin and cocaine, or crack. Used by about 7 million Americans, the two drugs cause more than 6,000 deaths annually. They are far more addictive than marijuana and create far greater damage to society in terms of health consequences, including AIDS, and crime. While marijuana clearly has many adverse effects, it causes fewer than one hundred fatalities a year even though 18 million Americans use it regularly.

This is not to suggest that marijuana is not harmful or should be legal. It is, however, necessary to recognize that intensive interdiction efforts have not reduced its availability or increased its cost, and that demand, which has declined, has done so largely in response to health concerns. A significant portion of federal drug law enforcement funds, including more than half the Coast Guard's $500 million budget, is directed toward marijuana inter-

diction. These resources might well be used more effectively for supply reduction efforts, education, and treatment
targeted at heroin and cocaine.

2. Maintain Illegal Status of Marijuana, Heroin, and Cocaine

Advocates of legalization argue that if marijuana, heroin,
and cocaine were legally available at reasonable cost, drug-
related crime would be eliminated. Government rather
than drug traffickers would profit from drug sales, and
funds now spent on law enforcement could be directed
toward education, prevention, and treatment.

For many reasons, legalization is not the answer. Any-
thing less than totally unlimited access will result in an
underground market with its attendant criminal activity
(as per the British experience). Yet few advocates of legalization contemplate unlimited distribution. Further, crimes
of violence caused by the effects of newly legalized drugs
would probably increase, particularly if crack use, which
produces erratic, violent behavior, becomes widespread.

Proponents of legalization actually recognize that it will
result in increased use. One cannot estimate the size of
the increase, but patterns for tobacco and alcohol use may
give some indication of the magnitude of the population
that legalization might produce. About 110 million Americans drink; 50 million smoke. Deaths attributable to alcohol are estimated at 100,000 a year; deaths from
smoking at 390,000. About 10 million Americans are alcoholics, while an additional 8 million have serious drinking problems.

Legalization would also signal a fundamental change
in American attitudes, reflecting social acceptance rather
than disapproval of drug use. Legalization would indicate
toleration at the threshold of first use, as children pattern
their behavior on the adults around them—parents,
teachers, and other role models. Because they are illegal,

cocaine, heroin, and marijuana are generally not used openly and are more difficult to obtain than tobacco and alcohol. Their illegality and the negative attitudes about their social use may have helped keep down the numbers of adolescents who have sampled them—considerably fewer than those who have tried alcohol and tobacco. Half the high school seniors surveyed in 1987 reported they tried marijuana, and 15 percent tried cocaine, but 67 percent smoked cigarettes and 92 percent tried alcohol.

The legality and social acceptability of alcohol and tobacco for adults make them sanctioned credentials of maturity that adolescents are impatient to attain. They are also readily available in the society, even with age restrictions on their sale. Their cost is very low when compared to illegal drugs (in some states a six-pack of beer costs less than a six-pack of cola). As a protection against this easy access, stronger legal barriers are beginning to emerge: higher drinking-age laws, stricter enforcement of no-sale-to-minor laws, and stringent no-smoking laws.

3. Reallocate Law Enforcement Resources

Drug law enforcement resources have more than tripled in the past eight years, from $800 million in 1981 to $2.5 billion in 1988. Drug law enforcement expenditures in 1989 will exceed $3.5 billion. There is little evidence, however, that law enforcement initiatives have cut drug availability in the United States.

A major review of drug interdiction, conducted in 1987 by the Rand Corporation, concluded that "increased drug interdiction efforts are not likely to greatly affect the availability of cocaine in the United States. Unless interdiction can very substantially increase the costs of smuggling, more effective interdiction will have modest effects on total cocaine consumption."[1] Since interdiction remains the largest component of the rapidly growing federal drug law enforcement effort, alternative uses of at least a portion of these funds should be explored.

Increased street-level enforcement, for example, may have more impact on retail cocaine prices than expanded interdiction efforts. The Rand study found that three-quarters of the cocaine profits are made at or near the street level; only 10 percent of the final cocaine price goes to those who produce coca or smuggle it into the United States. This suggests that arrests of low-level dealers may drive up the street cost of cocaine at the same time they help clean up neighborhoods plagued by drug dealing and violence. But there may also be negative consequences. Increased street-level enforcement in New York City, for example, has pushed drug dealers into other neighborhoods as well as overcrowding city jails. And a 1988 Rand study of drug abuse in Washington, D.C., found that, despite increased street-level drug arrests and convictions, drug-related violence and crime are increasing.[2]

Criminal justice systems in many cities are stretched far beyond capacity; overcrowded prisons release convicts early to take in new prisoners. Increased street-level enforcement would necessitate increased resources to expand the capacities of courts and prisons to cope with the growing numbers of drug arrests. Other approaches should perhaps be tried first. For example, drug treatment combined with urinalysis monitoring to make sure released offenders remain drug-free might prove a less costly and more effective alternative than incarceration.

There has been no systematic evaluation of drug law enforcement programs in the United States, so we do not yet know much about the relative effectiveness of various efforts or what mix works best for optimal results. The popular assumption about enforcement is that more resources will produce better results. (This reflects in part the historical notion that drug abuse is primarily a law enforcement problem and in part the political reality that "getting tough" on drug pushers is popular with the voters.) Some methods, however, are more effective than others; for example, seizures of dealers' assets as well as more intensive attacks on the complex money-laundering networks might work better than increased arrests.

Drug law enforcement must be an important part of any comprehensive national drug strategy, but it cannot by itself solve the nation's drug abuse problems. In the rapid buildup of enforcement resources since 1981, funding decisions have been based largely on intuition and political necessity. A careful, objective review of the entire range of enforcement initiatives is needed before it can be determined whether a reallocation of existing resources will substantially improve effectiveness. This review is particularly critical, since major additional enforcement resources are unlikely to be forthcoming.

B. INTERNATIONAL CONTROL EFFORTS

1. Give Drug Control Highest Diplomatic Priority

A comprehensive strategy to combat drug abuse must include a vigorous international component. Control efforts cannot be subordinated to other foreign policy concerns, as the Reagan administration appears to have done with the governments of Panama and Honduras. The United States must be willing to terminate economic assistance and other preferential treatment for drug source countries when all other efforts to develop cooperation have failed.[3]

To give higher foreign policy priority to drug control, Congress required the president in the Anti-Drug Abuse Act of 1986 to certify annually the adequacy of drug control cooperation by other governments. Failure to comply results in withholding trade concessions, foreign assistance, and U.S. support for World Bank and other loans. In the first two years under the new law, the United States "decertified" only countries with which bilateral relations were minimal—Laos, Afghanistan, Iran, and Syria. In 1988, under intense congressional pressure, President Reagan decertified Panama.

The certification process has the salutary effect of obliging U.S. government agencies to review international progress in narcotics control while sending a powerful message abroad that the United States gives the highest priority to cooperative efforts. However, the threat of decertification can strain complex and sensitive relations with countries like Mexico, which is now the single largest source of heroin and marijuana for the U.S. market.

Another dimension of an international narcotics control strategy involves addressing the broad social and economic aspects of the cocaine traffic. Since 1981, coca and cocaine have become critically important sources of foreign exchange for Colombia, Peru, and Bolivia. (Cocaine profits for Colombia in 1987 were about $1.5 billion, and for Bolivia and Peru, about $750 million each.)[4] The international recession of the early 1980s left these countries with massive debt burdens, making the economic imperative of cocaine traffic even greater. Only Colombia has been able to avoid rescheduling its foreign debt.

Since 1985, rapidly falling prices have reduced profits to coca farmers. In many areas they can now earn as much from growing food crops and should be encouraged to do so. Integrated rural development projects that create alternative sources of income for farmers growing drug crops should be an important part of international narcotics-control strategy.[5] Without providing alternatives, governments cannot succeed in suppressing the traffic.

An international strategy should explore new cooperative developmental initiatives as well, such as proposals to exchange debt for drug control. For countries like Peru and Bolivia, where the debt burden is the most pressing international concern, partial forgiveness could be an important incentive. In addition, an effort to set up alternative development programs would provide a means for the producer countries to wean their economies from dependence on coca cultivation and rebuild their capacity to participate in world credit markets.

2. Target Resources against Most Dangerous Drugs

As in domestic drug law enforcement, international control efforts undertaken by the United States should focus on heroin and cocaine as the most dangerous imports. Further efforts to limit marijuana entering the United States will have little impact, since domestic marijuana cultivation continues to expand. As the 1988 Rand Corporation study pointed out, attempts to limit foreign production of marijuana have served essentially to protect U.S. growers.

International efforts have received less than 2 percent of the total U.S. drug law enforcement funding in this decade, yet as much as a third of this small budget is spent on marijuana eradication and interdiction in Mexico, Colombia, Jamaica, Belize, and elsewhere. These scant resources should be concentrated against cocaine and heroin production.

3. Develop a More Flexible, Comprehensive International Strategy

An international drug control strategy must be sufficiently flexible to develop new responses quickly. Eradication programs, which proved successful against opium in the 1970s with Turkey and Mexico, have not worked against rapidly expanding coca cultivation in Peru, Bolivia, and Colombia in the 1980s.

The continuing failure to identify an effective coca herbicide combined with the reluctance of these governments to permit eradication makes progress unlikely. New initiatives should be found that do not rely on eradication, which, even if possible, would have only a marginal effect on the price of cocaine in the United States.[6]

Eradication, however, need not be completely abandoned as part of a comprehensive strategy. If Mexico's new government under President Carlos Salinas de Gortari makes drug eradication a priority and full cooperation with the United States is reestablished, Mexico's role as a supplier could again significantly diminish. Eradication may also become an effective means for producing countries to address their own growing drug abuse problems.[7]

4. Give Greater Support to Regional and Multilateral Drug Control Efforts

The United States should pursue a multilateral approach to combating drug abuse and traffic. Despite its public statements about the importance of international cooperation, the Reagan administration pursued a unilateral course, defining both the problem and the program in terms of U.S. interests. As a result, the drug-producing countries had few incentives to reduce production. For example, the use of U.S. military forces in "Operation Blastfurnace" to curtail cocaine production in Bolivia in 1987 was viewed by many Latin Americans as interventionist and thus increased serious political resistance to all drug control efforts. It may also have added to the difficulty of gaining support for the longer-term effort to eradicate coca.

Instead of using the American military or the U.S. Drug Enforcement Administration to help foreign governments fight drug traffickers, the United States should promote the creation of a drug agency within the United Nations to provide operational enforcement assistance. Such an agency would provide a more acceptable political alternative for producer countries and the United States, and might also prove more effective.

Multilateral efforts are increasingly necessary, as traffickers have the resources and power to shift their operations from one country to another. For example, money laundering in offshore banks requires close cooperation among many governments. As banking codes in the Netherlands Antilles and Bahamas have become more stringent, Panama has emerged as the most frequently used illicit banking center, actively protected by General Manuel Noriega. Multilateral or regional efforts to curtail these transactions would probably be more promising than unilateral U.S. initiatives.

The United States should actively support the Inter-American Committee on Drug Abuse of the Organization of American States, recently created to deal with drug production and trafficking in Latin America. The UN drug agencies also should receive greater U.S. support; instead, U.S. contributions to the United Nations Fund for Drug Abuse Control (UNFDAC) have actually decreased.

C. DEMAND REDUCTION–PREVENTION AND EDUCATION

1. Encourage Different Initiatives to Meet Different Needs

The most promising prevention efforts are currently concentrated on school curricula designed to teach life skills that help children resist tobacco, alcohol, and drug use. Their effect on inner-city, minority schoolchildren is only now being tested. However, many of the young people most at risk do not attend school. For them, drug-prevention efforts must be integrated into community programs that are intended to provide broader social support as well.

Prevention programs should also be tailored to reflect regional and ethnic differences. National surveys on illicit drug use give an overall picture of trends within the general population but do not illuminate definite regional and local variations. In Washington, D.C., for example, PCP is a major problem, while in Los Angeles and other southwestern cities, inhalants (glue sniffing) are widely used.

Moreover, local communities should be encouraged to develop their own prevention initiatives, both because they know what their immediate problems are and because local residents are more likely to work to improve their own neighborhoods by driving out drug abuse and street traffic.

The federal government can strengthen these efforts by creating a nationwide network to share information and initiatives. In many communities where there is a pervasive sense of helplessness, federal support to local groups willing to organize community prevention efforts can be critical to any long-term national strategy.

2. Expand the Media Campaign to Change Attitudes about Drug Use

Advertising is a powerful force in shaping American attitudes about desirable behavior. The antismoking ads required by the Federal Communications Commission to counter cigarette advertising from 1967 through 1970 resulted in a decline in cigarette consumption of 10 percent, the first time this century that smoking declined for more than two consecutive years. When cigarette and antismoking ads were removed from the airwaves in 1971, cigarette consumption resumed its upward trend.[8]

The national advertising campaign launched by the Partnership for a Drug-Free America a year ago shows positive initial results in changing attitudes about illicit drug use in areas where the ads are frequently aired. However, because the campaign relies entirely on donated time, it has not achieved widespread coverage. A national drug-prevention strategy should expand the Partnership's efforts by providing incentives to attract additional contributions from advertisers and the media— for example, tax relief for contributors and/or matching federal funds to purchase airtime. As the antismoking ads demonstrated, a long-term commitment to advertising is required to maintain whatever positive impact it has in changing behavior.

3. Use Social Policy to Reinforce Prevention

Social policy establishes the limits of acceptable behavior at least as much as legislative policy. Laws that restrict drug use are most effective when there is national consensus to support them. When social policy reinforces the legal prohibitions and there is reduced tolerance for drug or alcohol abuse, the impact is felt by students or children even when they are not in school, and by adults as well.

Growing public concern about safety in the workplace and especially on the highways, for example, has led to stricter drinking laws as well as campaigns by groups like Mothers Against Drunk Driving (MADD). Social tolerance for driving while intoxicated has greatly declined in recent years. In the workplace, drug testing has become a means both for deterring and detecting drug use, as well as a way to send a clear message, particularly to young people preparing for employment, that drug use will not be tolerated.

4. Make Prevention and Education Research a High Priority

Prevention research has received far less support even than prevention itself and education—which together accounted for only 1 percent of total federal drug expenditures from 1982 through 1986. As a result of this chronic neglect, very little is known about what works to prevent drug use. It will take several years to develop carefully structured research programs that will lead to effective, long-term prevention strategies. In addition to evaluating program models, research should explore why young people move from experimenting with drugs to becoming chronic users. Although the vast majority of teenagers try alcohol and drugs, only 5 to 15 percent of them will become compulsive abusers who put themselves at high risk.[9] And despite the ready availability of drugs in the inner city, many minority young people do not become involved with them. It is important to learn more about what internal and external factors help them resist an increasingly dominant culture. Understanding the process that leads certain adolescents and not others to adopt destructive behaviors could be important in developing more effective prevention and intervention strategies.

D. DEMAND REDUCTION—TREATMENT

1. Provide Treatment on Demand

NIDA believes that publicly funded drug treatment programs are currently available for only 4 percent of the 6.5 million people who are severely dependent on drugs. The American Medical Association (AMA) estimates that only 150,000 of the nation's 1.3 million intravenous drug users are receiving treatment. In 1988, President Reagan's AIDS Commission recommended that $15 billion be spent over the next ten years for treatment services. In the same year, Congress authorized $1.6 billion for treatment in the Anti-Drug Abuse Act, but appropriated only $880 million for 1989. Additional resources will be needed if treatment on demand is to become a reality.

Making treatment resources easily accessible to those who need them is critically important. Since many addicts are reluctant to seek treatment, bureaucratic and geographic obstacles should be minimized. The AMA board of trustees recently recommended changes in federal regulations to permit doctors to treat heroin addicts with methadone in their offices rather than in public clinics. This would give addicts greater privacy as well as more flexibility in finding a conveniently located doctor. In addition, by allowing doctors to treat addicts, the proposal would immediately expand the availability of methadone treatment.

Other new ways of delivering treatment services must also be developed. Traditionally, providers have included clinics, hospitals, residential therapeutic communities, and outpatient programs. Experiments are under way with new models—for example, mobile methadone clinics, more acceptable to the community and more convenient for the addicts. Or programs to bring treatment to homeless addicts, offering temporary housing and intensive counseling after initial, medically supervised detoxification. Program participants must remain free of drugs and alcohol, which are monitored by random urine testing. Initial results of this experiment in Portland, Oregon, are promising: six months after leaving the program, half the participants remain drug-free. City officials note that the monthly cost is $165 person, substantially lower than other types of residential programs.

2. Make Treatment Research a High Priority

The Reagan administration's cuts in demand reduction funding devastated treatment research. There are few controlled studies on treatment effectiveness, and very little work has been done on new types of treatments generated in response to changing drug abuse patterns. Yet new models of treatment are urgently needed for many different types of addicts, including adolescents, women who are single parents, and crack users. And untested but promising treatment models, like acupuncture to reduce crack cravings, must be systematically evaluated.

Recent studies indicate that matching patients with treatment modalities can significantly improve the outcome for about 60 percent of the patient population. About 20 percent benefit from treatment of any kind. But for most, greater awareness of patient-program matching could lead to a more efficient use of resources.

Research is also needed to develop ways of reaching drug abusers with severe psychiatric problems (about one-fifth of the patient population). Recent studies have found that they do not respond well to any treatment[10] and are often the most dangerous. Clinicians believe that this group is growing, particularly since the emergence of crack, making it urgent that new treatments be found.

Research into the biomedical bases of addiction is essential for understanding the physiological nature of addiction and for developing pharmacological responses, including a "blocker" for the effects of cocaine. (Methadone has been used for twenty-five years to block the effects of heroin, but the issue is whether abstinence or substitution should be the goal.) As work with children of alcoholics has shown, research can illuminate the genetic and behavioral aspects of addiction and help identify at an early age those who are at high risk.

Because research rarely produces immediate, highly visible results in the war on drugs, it has not received sustained political support. But without assured funding, long-term research cannot be undertaken. Hundreds of millions of treatment dollars will be wasted unless programs are systematically evaluated and refined. A strong commitment to research must be central to any national drug strategy.

3. Concentrate Treatment Resources in the Criminal Justice System

Research confirms that criminal offenders are more deeply involved in drug abuse than any other group in the population, yet treatment programs for them are extremely rare. The current crisis of prison overcrowding has focused attention on the need to develop programs to treat offenders and monitor their drug use after their release.

A few programs do exist. Some prisons have Alcoholics Anonymous and Narcotics Anonymous meetings; some have counseling groups; a few have drug-free residential programs. Although there has been very little systematic research on them, one that has been studied is "Stay'N Out," a therapeutic community program operating in two New York prisons. The results are promising. Prisoners who participated in the year-long program and continued with drug programs after release were half as likely to be arrested or commit parole violations three years later as those who did not take part.[11]

In addition to expanding treatment for criminal offenders, drug treatment and supervision programs should be explored as an alternative to incarceration, both before trial as well as during probation and parole. Drug testing is now being used in some jurisdictions to determine whether arrested offenders should be released before trial.

The prospect of staying out of jail may give some detained drug abusers a powerful motive for giving up drugs and entering treatment as a condition of release. Regular testing can deter drug use among offenders on pretrial release, probation, or parole, when positive evidence will result in immediate incarceration or re-incarceration. Drug testing, however, while useful as a means of assessing risk, is not by itself likely to change behavior over the longer term. Ongoing treatment programs must be available in order to break the cycle of crime and drug abuse.

4. Collaborate with the Private Sector in Developing Cost-effective Treatment

Because of inadequate federal support for treatment research, not much is known about the relative effectiveness of publicly funded drug treatment programs, and even less is known about private programs. Very few have been objectively evaluated. Yet businesses and insurance companies spend hundreds of millions of dollars each year to provide drug treatment for their employees, usually in residential programs covered by insurance premiums. As more testing is done in the workplace, more employees are likely to need help.

Because the demand for treatment has grown faster than the availability of private programs, neither employers nor insurance providers have subjected the available programs to careful scrutiny. However, soaring insurance costs are now forcing companies to take a closer look at what their treatment dollars are buying. The Betty Ford Center in California, for example, charges about $6,000 for residential treatment, which lasts about one month. Hazelden, in Minnesota, charges $5,000. Yet other institutions, like Fair Oaks Hospital in New Jersey, and Regent Hospital in New York City, charge as much as $30,000 for one month's treatment.

Government and industry in partnership should undertake independent evaluations of the performance of these rehabilitation programs. Federal efforts to develop effective models for publicly funded treatment programs could benefit from knowing what works in the private sector, where funding has not been as limited. Evaluation could also lead to considerable savings in tax dollars and insurance premiums. Under present federal tax law, employers can deduct all insurance premiums, thereby lowering their taxes. However, their tax savings are always less than the cost of premiums. Some experts estimate that if employer write-offs were limited to $6,000 for each drug abuse treatment, additional taxes of $5 to $8 billion would have been paid by businesses in the past eight years.[12]

CONCLUSION

A comprehensive national drug strategy should set as its primary goal the reduction of illicit drug use, recognizing the impossibility of eliminating all use. Like the war against cancer, the war against drugs will need a long-term commitment to prevention, education, treatment, and research. It will also need a substantial law enforcement effort. Within this multilayered approach, the effectiveness of each component must be carefully assessed. Until now, the absence of any systematic evaluation of antidrug programs has rendered strategic planning ineffective while millions of dollars have been wasted as the drug crisis has deepened.

The politicians' response to public concern about drug abuse, particularly before national elections, has been to vote more money and tougher penalties without reflecting on goals and priorities. However, there should be an active debate involving Congress, the executive branch, the medical and law enforcement communities, and the public about what we want to achieve. Budget constraints make large additional resources unlikely and priorities imperative.

At present we have little empirical basis for deciding how public resources should be allocated between supply reduction and demand reduction programs or among enforcement initiatives. Filling those knowledge gaps is a critically important first step.

After almost a decade of neglect, demand reduction has reemerged as an important element of a national policy. The current enthusiasm for prevention and education as the answer to drug abuse carries with it the danger that if these programs fail to produce quick results—as is likely because we know only very little about what works— demand reduction will again lose favor. Prevention and treatment efforts may take years before they make a difference. The same is true for research, which is as important in combating drug abuse as it is in the fight against cancer. It too must be protected against the vagaries of the political cycle if lasting results are to be achieved.

Progress against drug abuse will be slow and uneven. There are no easy answers or quick fixes, but there are promising developments on a number of fronts that could lead to real reductions in drug use and abuse over the long term.

For years, our society thought of drug abuse primarily as a moral issue, reflecting a personal failure of will as well as a violation of criminal law. Only now are Americans beginning to understand that the problem is far more complex, involving not only individual behavior but also fundamental issues of poverty and opportunity. Historically, the United States has operated at its best in times of crisis in responding to major challenges. We are now faced with a drug crisis that demands a commitment and a strategy as comprehensive as the country's successful responses to national emergencies in the past. Ultimately, America's strength and competitiveness in future decades will require such a commitment, such a national strategy.

Notes

Chapter 2

1. L. D. Johnston et al., *Illicit Drug Use, Smoking & Drinking by America's High School Students, College Students & Young Adults 1975-1987* (Rockville, Md.: National Institute on Drug Abuse, 1988).

2. National Institute on Drug Abuse, *1985 Household Survey* (Rockville, Md.: 1987). According to the most recent National Household Survey on Drug Abuse conducted in 1985, 62 million Americans have tried marijuana; 22 million have tried cocaine. Nearly one in ten (18.2 million) used marijuana within the month before the survey, compared to six in ten who used alcohol and three in ten who smoked cigarettes.

3. A 1988 survey of the 1,000 biggest companies by the Mercer Meidinger Hansen division of Marsh & McLennan Companies, a Chicago insurance firm.

4. Information is derived from two primary sources: the annual High School Senior Survey conducted by the University of Michigan's Institute for Social Research and the periodic National Household Survey on Drug Abuse sponsored by the National Institute of Drug Abuse.

The focus of the two national surveys is on drug use rather than abuse. They report on frequency of use—whether a respondent has ever used a drug, whether in the last year, the last month, or daily within the last month.

Information on drug abuse comes primarily from two other nationwide sources: the Drug Abuse Warning Network (DAWN), which reports drug overdoses and deaths from hospital emergency room admissions and medical examiner cases; and the

Client Oriented Data Acquisition Process (CODAP), which provides information on persons entering publicly funded drug abuse treatment programs. Until 1981, states were required as a condition of federal funding to report CODAP information; since then, under the federal government's block grant funding, which gives states broad discretion, client treatment reporting has been voluntary and much less comprehensive.

5. Johnston, *Illicit Drug Use*, 1988.

6. Hospital emergency room admissions linked to cocaine jumped 86 percent in 1987—from 24,847 in 1986 to 46,331. Smoking cocaine has increased dramatically as a proportion of these cocaine-related admissions. In 1987, DAWN reported that 30 percent of the cocaine cases involved smoking, probably crack, as compared to 10 percent in 1985, the first year crack appeared on the streets. These trends are confirmed by various treatment programs. At Phoenix House, New York City's largest residential drug treatment program, for example, cocaine was the drug of choice of 30 percent of those entering treatment in 1984. By 1986, that figure had doubled.

7. The number of women seeking treatment for cocaine and crack at Phoenix House in New York City more than doubled from 1985 to 1987. More than a third of the crack addicts admitted to publicly funded drug treatment programs in New York State in 1987 were women.

8. S. N. MacGregor et al., "Cocaine Use during Pregnancy: Adverse Perinatal Outcome," *American Journal of Obstetrics and Gynecology* 157, no. 3 (September 1987): 686–90.

9. A major national survey by the U.S. Justice Department in 1987 found that illicit drug use is far more extensive among those arrested for felony offenses than previously believed. The survey used objective urinalysis testing data for 2,000 men in twelve cities shortly following their arrest. New York City had the highest percentage of drug users among those detained at 79 percent; Washington, D.C., was second at 77 percent; and Phoenix was lowest at 53 percent.

The study also confirmed the rapid spread of cocaine use, particularly since the emergence of crack. Among those arrested for serious crimes in New York City, cocaine use had almost doubled since 1984; in Washington, D.C., it more than tripled. This pattern was reflected in the other cities as well, with cocaine substantially more prevelant than either heroin or marijuana.

10. Nationwide, arrests for possession of heroin and/or cocaine jumped from 49,000 in 1981 to 295,000 in 1987; during the same period, arrests for sales increased from 24,000 to 132,000.

In New York, serious crimes (robbery, assault, and homicide), which had fallen steadily between 1981 and 1986, increased 5.6 percent in 1986 and 3.4 percent in 1987. Aggravated assaults in 1987 jumped 12.1 percent and murders 5.8 percent; in 1986, murders increased 18 percent. Felony drug arrests almost doubled since 1984; convictions more than tripled. Police officials attribute these increases to crack—to the need to acquire money for drugs as well as to the irrational behavior while under their influence.

In Washington, D.C., the drug-related crime rate increased 15 percent in 1988. Killings more than doubled; the city's prison population increased more than 50 percent in the last five years.

In New Jersey, drug-related arrests went from 40,000 in 1986 to 66,000 in 1988. Smaller cities are also experiencing a surge in drug-related crime. In Hartford, for example, a city of 138,000, drug-related arrests jumped from 576 in 1986 to more than 1,500 in 1988.

11. New York City—386 drug arrests in 1983; 1,052 in 1987; Washington, D.C.—483 in 1983; 1,894 in 1987; Los Angeles—41 in 1980; 1,719 in 1987.

Chapter 2, Appendix

1. Media-Advertising Partnership for a Drug-Free America, *Changing Attitudes Toward Drug Use, 1988* (Rochester, N.Y.: Gordon S. Black Corporation).

2. A. Blanken, E. Adams, J. Durell, "Drug Abuse: Implications and Trends," *Psychiatric Medicine* 3, no. 3 (1987).

3. DAWN 1976-1985, topical data from DAWN, Statistical Series H, no. 3, National Institute on Drug Abuse (1987).

4. Blanken, "Drug Abuse," 1987.

Chapter 3

1. David Musto, *The American Disease: Origins of Narcotics Control* (New Haven: Yale University Press, 1973).

2. An instructive contrast to U.S. drug policy exists in several European countries where drug abuse has also become a major concern during the past two decades. In general, the European approach emphasizes health concerns—treatment and prevention—rather than law enforcement, although that has become a greater concern in recent years. The three countries discussed here—Sweden, Great Britain, and the Netherlands—have, however, all focused on very different aspects of the problem.

Sweden has adopted a highly restrictive policy intended to create a drug-free society. It depends on widespread public support as well as strict enforcement of severe laws prohibiting all forms of drug possession. Clearly, the system is working: surveys of young men entering compulsory military service in 1980 found that almost 20 percent of them had tried an illicit drug; in 1986, the figure had dropped to 7 percent. Hans Lundborg, "The European Experience," working paper, Bilateral Commission on the Future of U.S.-Mexican Relations (Ford Foundation, New York, 1987).

Sweden provides extensive prevention and treatment resources and is particularly concerned with the spread of AIDS among intravenous drug users. Addicts are treated in special public health clinics that provide intensive residential and aftercare services. (Experiments in the late 1960s to give legal prescriptions of amphetamines were abandoned. Instead of reducing widespread amphetamine addiction, the illegal sales of prescriptions expanded the addict population.)

The primary drug problem in Great Britain is heroin addiction, despite a recent increase in cocaine and amphetamine abuse. Traditionally, the British viewed addiction more as a medical than a law enforcement problem; however, that view has changed in recent years as drug abuse became more widespread.

In the two decades following World War II, British doctors were permitted to prescribe heroin. The principal motive underlying this approach was to reduce criminality among addicts and to provide some medical supervision. But heroin addiction increased, and a black market in heroin developed, leading to a new system under which heroin could be prescribed and dispensed only at drug clinics. By the early 1970s, the majority of addicts were placed on methadone maintenance as a substitute for heroin. (Today, fewer than one hundred addicts are given heroin legally while more than seven thousand are given methadone.)

In the Netherlands, the Dutch government has treated drug abuse primarily as a health and social welfare problem. Treatment and prevention programs take precedence over law enforcement, and high priority is given to improving the health of drug addicts. Methadone is widely prescribed for heroin addicts, and needle-exchange programs have been initiated to contain the spread of the AIDS virus.

Heroin is not legally available. A proposal by the city of Amsterdam to distribute free heroin to addicts was rejected by the Dutch government. Marijuana use, however, is openly tolerated, although the sale of marijuana is still illegal. A brief experiment in selling marijuana at local youth centers ended after extensive protests from other European countries. Severe penalties are imposed on major drug traffickers.

In general, European countries are moving toward stricter drug laws and stricter enforcement. Nonetheless, consumption, especially of cocaine but also of heroin, has increased as drug traffickers seek new markets to absorb expanding worldwide production. Even so, the level of drug abuse in Western Europe remains substantially lower than in the United States. This may reflect the impact of different cultural traditions and values, as well as the long-term impact of focusing on drug prevention, treatment, and education rather than on law enforcement.

3. P. Reuter, G. Crawford, J. Cave, *Sealing the Borders* (Santa Monica, Calif.: Rand Corporation, 1988).

4. "New York's Drug Commander," *The New York Times*, March 12, 1989.

5. U.S. Government Accounting Office, *Drug Abuse Prevention* (GAO/HRD-88-26), Washington, D.C., December 1987

6. The Office of Management and Budget (OMB) currently estimates that about $4.6 billion will be spent for drug programs in 1989. Of this amount, about $1.2 billion will support demand reduction efforts, a one-third increase over the previous year. Congress must now decide whether or where to find additional sources of funding to meet the full $2.75 billion authorized under the 1988 act.

Chapter 3, Appendix 1

1. J. Van Wert, "Mexican Narcotics Control: A Decade of Institutionalization and a Matter for Diplomacy," *Anales del Colegio de Mexico* (December 1986).

2. Reuter, Crawford, and Cave, *Sealing the Borders*, 1988.

Chapter 4

1. See Brian R. Flay et al., "Are Social-Psychological Smoking Prevention Programs Effective? The Waterloo Study," *Journal of Behavioral Medicine* 8, no. 1 (1985): 37-59, for a good summary of prevention programs.

2. J. M. Polich et al., *Strategies for Controlling Adolescent Drug Use* (Santa Monica, Calif.: Rand Corporation, 1984).

3. Follow-up studies have found that programs like the Life Skills Training Program developed at Cornell University Medical College can reduce new cigarette smoking by teenagers by half, whether the program is implemented by outside health professionals, peers, or by regular classroom teachers. Students who received "booster sessions" in the second year of the study showed an 87 percent reduction in new smoking compared to schools not participating in the program. The program also improved assertiveness and self-esteem. See Gil S. Botvin, "Prevention of Adolescent Substance Abuse through the Development of Personal and Social Competence," *Preventing Adolescent Drug Abuse: Intervention Strategies*, NIDA Research Monograph 47 (Washington, D.C.: Department of Health and Human Services, 1985).

One of the most rigorous tests of the social-influences approach to smoking prevention, conducted by the University of Waterloo in Ontario, Canada, found that the program was most effective for students at high risk—those who had parents, friends, and siblings who smoked. Among such students, 78 percent of the experimental group remained nonsmokers, compared to 44 percent of those in the control group. Further, the prevention results were monitored for several years: 60 percent of the experimental group who had begun the program in sixth grade were still nonsmokers at the end of the eighth grade, compared to 47 percent of the control group. (Flay, "Are Social-Psychological Smoking Prevention Programs Effective?" 1985.)

These programs, targeted at sixth- and seventh-graders, had positive and measurable results in primary prevention at the age when experimental smoking usually begins. Nonsmoking behavior also persists for several years. This is particularly significant, since researchers believe that the longer children delay using tobacco and alcohol, the less likely they will be to develop serious drug use problems. A delay of even two or three years can provide valuable time for intellectual and social development that can strengthen the teenager's capacity to decide not to use drugs. Ninety percent of those who smoke, for example, begin by age nineteen.

4. Denise B. Kandel and J. A. Logan, "Patterns of Drug Abuse from Adolescence to Young Adulthood: I. Periods of Risk for Initiation, Continued Use, and Discontinuation," *American Journal of Public Health* 74, no. 7 (1984): 660-66.

5. Several major studies are now evaluating the effectivenss of the Life Skills Training program with urban minority schoolchildren in New York and New Jersey. Another study is testing the social-influences approach in schools in Kansas and Indiana; the same curricula are being used in both suburban and inner-city schools. Project Alert, a major seven-year study of prevention curricula conducted by the Rand Corporation, is looking at the impact of social influences and life skills training on a wide range of seventh-grade schoolchildren, including minorities, in Oregon and California.

6. Parents Who Care, based in California, is a typical program. It organizes drug-free social activities and holds older peer orientations for eighth-graders, providing them with role models who assure them they do not have to drink or use drugs to be socially acceptable. Teens Who Care does the same.

7. Media-Advertising Partnership for a Drug-Free America, *The Attitudinal Basis of Drug Use* (Rochester, N.Y.: Gordon S. Black Corporation, 1987).

8. Estimates obtained from National Association of State Alcohol and Drug Abuse Directors, Washington, D.C.

9. D. D. Simpson and S. B. Sells, "Effectiveness of Treatment for Drug Abuse," *Advances in Alcohol and Substance Abuse* 2, no. 1 (1982): 7-29.

10. Studies have shown that more than two-thirds of the pa-

tients who enter maintenance programs remain in methadone treatment for a year or more and that during this time there is a dramatic reduction in crimes committed and an increase in gainful employment. Intravenous drug use also decreases dramatically. A recent study of heroin addicts in methadone programs in New York, Philadelphia, and Baltimore found that 71 percent of those who remained in treatment for one year or more had stopped intravenous drug use; of those who left the programs, 82 percent quickly resumed the habit. (J. C. Ball et al., "Reducing the Risks of AIDS through Methadone Maintenance," *Journal of Health and Social Behavior* 29, no. 3 (September 1988).

11. G. De Leon and S. Schwartz, "Therapeutic Communities: What Are the Retention Rates?" *American Journal of Drug and Alcohol Abuse* 10, no. 2 (1984): 267-84.

12. G. De Leon, H. Wexler, and N. Jainchill, "The Therapeutic Community: Success and Improvement Rates 5 Years after Treatment," *International Journal of the Addictions* 17, no. 4 (1982): 703-47.

13. Cocaine Anonymous was founded in 1982 and now has more than a thousand groups nationwide.

14. C. P. O'Brien, "Treatment Research, Second Triennial Report on Drug Abuse and Drug Abuse Research," DHHS pub. no. (ADM) 87-1486, Washington, D.C., 1987.

15. "Breaking the Cycle of Addiction," *Science*, August 26, 1988, pp. 1029-30.

16. Polich et al., *Strategies for Controlling Adolescent Drug Use*, 1984.

17. Only 5 percent of the 3,000 publicly supported treatment facilities surveyed by NIDA and NIAAA in 1982 served a predominantly adolescent population.

18. R. L. Hubbard et al., "Characteristics, Behaviors, and Outcomes for Youth in the Treatment Outcome Prospective Study," *Treatment Services for Adolescent Substance Abusers*, NIDA Research Monograph Series (Washington, D.C.: Department of Health and Human Services, 1985).

19. A nationwide survey in 1985 by Metropolitan Life Insurance Company found that private treatment for substance abuse was provided overwhelmingly in residential hospital settings.

No other claims category, including pregnancy and birth, showed a higher rate of hospitalization. The survey also found that treatment for substance abuse in a specialized facility generally took 24.6 days and cost an average of $7,186 per confinement.

20. Foster Higgins Health Care Benefits Survey (Princeton, N.J., 1987).

21. A 1988 survey of 7,500 businesses by the Department of Labor's Bureau of Labor Statistics found that more than half of those with 5,000 or more employees had drug-testing programs. The federal government has instituted broad-scale testing in the military and a number of federal agencies, including the Department of Transportation, the Central Intelligence Agency, and the Department of Health and Human Services. Additional testing is planned in 1989 for 346,000 federal workers in sensitive jobs in forty-two agencies. By the end of 1989, the government will require testing of four million private transportation workers, including airline pilots, truck drivers, and railroad engineers.

22. E. Wish and B. Johnson, "The Impact of Substance Abuse in Criminal Careers," in *Criminal Careers and Career Criminals*, ed. A. Blumstein et al. (Washington, D.C.: National Academy Press, 1986).

Chapter 5

1. P. Reuter, G. Crawford, J. Cave, *Sealing the Borders* (Santa Monica, Calif.: Rand Corporation, 1988).

2. P. Reuter et al., *Drug Use and Drug Programs in the Washington Metropolitan Area* (Santa Monica, Calif.: Rand Corporation, 1988).

3. We have done so only once, in 1980, when the Bolivian government was taken over by General Garcia Meza, who was closely linked to the cocaine traffic. The United States refused to recognize the regime and terminated all assistance. Other governments, regional organizations, and international financial institutions supported U.S. efforts. In 1982, the Bolivian military turned power over to a democratically elected president, and U.S. assistance resumed.

4. *The Economist*, October 8, 1988, p. 21.

5. The United States spends only 3 percent of its international

narcotics control program budget, about $3 million a year, on narcotics-related development assistance worldwide.

6. Reuter, Crawford, and Cave *(Sealing the Borders,* 1988) estimated that the costs of coca cultivation and cocaine refining constitute about 2 percent of the street price of cocaine in the United States and that if eradication cut coca production by half, U.S. prices would increase by less than 1 percent.

7. In Colombia, for example, *basuco,* a form of coca paste that is highly addictive, has created a major drug problem among young people. Coca production is expanding not only because of U.S. demand but also to supply this new domestic market. In Pakistan, opium production is being driven by the country's rapidly growing number of heroin addicts, now estimated to exceed 150,000. As a result, Pakistan undertook aerial herbicidal eradication in 1987 for the first time. In Thailand heroin addiction is also increasing, and with assistance from the UN, the United States, and other countries, the Thai government is now eradicating opium as well as developing income-substitution programs for the opium-growing hill tribes.

8. K. Warner, "The Effects of Publicity and Policy on Smoking and Health," *Business and Health,* November 1984, pp. 7-13.

9. A. Friedman, "Referral and Diagnosis of Adolescent Substance Abusers," *Treatment Services for Adolescent Substance Abusers,* NIDA Research Monograph Series (Washington, D.C.: Department of Health and Human Services, 1985).

10. A. T. McLellan et al., "New Data from the Addiction Severity Index," *Journal of Nervous and Mental Disease* 173 (1985): 412-23.

11. H. Wexler et al., *A Model Prison Rehabilitation Program: An Evaluation of the "Stay'N Out" Therapeutic Community* (New York: Narcotic & Drug Research, Inc., 1988).

12. T. Cohen, "Why Subsidize Expensive Programs?" *The New York Times,* June 6, 1988, p. A23.

Index